PURPOSEFUL HUSTLE

DEANNA SINGH

www.deannasingh.com

Purposeful Hustle
Direct Your Life's Work Towards Making a Positive Impact
Copyrighted © 2018 Deanna Singh
ISBN: 978-1-948365-41-3
Library of Congress Number: 2018947656
First Edition

For information, please contact:
Deanna Singh
www.deannasingh.com
info@deannasingh.com

Cover design by Ferris Brennan and Deanna Singh

DEANNA SINGH
UPLIFTING IMPACT
WWW.DEANNASINGH.COM - MILWAUKEE, WI

DEDICATED TO:

Bachan and Patricia Singh, who taught me
how to serve others and fight for things bigger than myself.

Zephaniah and Zion Singh Ponder who I am certain will become
some of the greatest Purposeful Hustlers the world has ever known.

Justin Ponder, a great teacher, friend and the love of my life.
It is a privilege to build a life of purpose with you.

TABLE OF CONTENTS

Introduction

Be who God meant you to be and you
will set the world on fire.

-St. Catherine of Siena

"**H**ow do I use my talents, skills, or resources to have a greater impact?" This is the core question I've seen emerge time and again during my countless conversations with people from all walks of life. The people who have approached me are a microcosm of the beautiful demographics that make up humankind—people of different ages, races, education levels, faiths, and genders. I can see the pain in their eyes as they talk about how they desperately want to make an impact in the world. They talk about how they want to be more deeply involved in social justice. They are frustrated by what they hear and disgusted by what they see. And they want to channel that frustration and disgust into something productive—something that will yield a greater future.

These beautiful souls come to me with the question, "How do I use my talents, skills, and resources to have a greater impact?" because I have managed to consistently align my life's work with making a positive impact. Though I have worked in many different fields, my focus has always centered around creating profound change at the individual, family, and community level. I find it encouraging that others yearn to know how they, too, can make a positive difference in the world.

I love talking to people about how they can shift their life toward greater impact. I love sharing what I have learned along the way. I love hearing about people's aspirations for creating change. I also understand how hard it is to live in a purposeful way that truly engages in big change. There are not a lot of resources on how to live a purposeful lifestyle, so when I talk with others, I try to equip them with the lessons I've learned throughout my personal journey. My life's path has curved this way and that and has been full of ruts and obstacles. Along the way I have had to build up a toolkit of resources, lessons learned, and roadmaps that I've used to effectively live in the service of others and pursue my purpose in life. This toolkit has been vital in my work and I willingly share it with those who are sick of being on the sidelines of social injustice and want to be a part of a healthy change.

My conversations with these purpose-seeking individuals are always rewarding experiences because we both leave feeling reinvigorated about the possibilities for a brighter future. The inquirer's questions, drive, and commitment to social justice are humbling and inspiring. I relish the opportunity to help the people who come to me because I know that if they figure out their purpose, there is no limit to the good they can accomplish. I always hope that by the end of our conversations they will walk away with some lessons from my journey and a few new tools to forge their own path.

If I had to sum up the most significant lesson I have learned, it is that to be an effective change maker, you have to blend intentional thought (Purpose), with intentional action (Hustle). Thus the term, Purposeful Hustle. Purposeful Hustle is directing your life's work toward intentionally making a positive impact in the world. Therefore, a Purposeful Hustler is someone who exists in the world with the ultimate goal of creating positive change.

I hope this book fills a void on how to blend purpose with hustle. I hope it will provide you with the guidance you need to do what I have been able to do, but much better!

"**P**urposeful Hustle is directing your life's work toward intentionally making a positive impact in the world. Therefore, a Purposeful Hustler is someone who exists in the world with the ultimate goal of creating positive change."

I currently state my purpose simply as: "Shifting power to marginalized communities." What does that mean? It means that everything I do has to come back to that purpose. Because I am very vocal about my purpose, I was asked by a friend how this book connected back to it. I firmly believe that unless we have more people working in their purposes, we are not going to have enough strength to do the work that must be done to bring about peace and equity in the world. I am hoping that by writing this book, sharing my experiences, and helping others find the courage to become activated, we will be able to gain more traction in the social justice space. Together, I am confident we can disrupt the current power paradigm. My other hope is that this book will act as a blueprint for change that I can use to train others across the country. Is that a lofty goal? Yes, but because it is within my purpose I am okay with that!

How did I arrive at my current stated purpose? Through both my upbringing and a windy, eclectic career. A lot of people talk about their career using a linear road or a ladder, but mine has been more complicated than that. My twisting life path has allowed me to accumulate a host of experiences, all revolving around my Purposeful Hustle. These experiences have positioned me as an "expert in impact," someone others seek when they want to figure out how to make their own impact. This journey started humbly, in Milwaukee, Wisconsin.

I grew up in a loving family that worked their hands to the bone so I could go off to college (in their minds, that's what all successful people did) and do great things. No pressure. My father was an immigrant from a small village in India who barely spoke English. My mother was one of nine children raised in the housing projects of Milwaukee by a single mother. They both started with very little and grew a reality that far surpassed what any statistic would have predicted. They showed me what is possible when marginalized people, those who society has discounted because of socioeconomic status, have power. Instead of succumbing to society's expectations, they made themselves into positive statistics and managed to change their own life trajectories, as well as the trajectories of their family. Through their example, they helped lay the groundwork for my core purpose in life, which is to use my time, talents, and opportunities to shift power to marginalized communities. To me, there is nothing as rewarding as helping people realize their dreams.

Though my parents planted the seeds that would eventually blossom into my purpose, I didn't fully develop or think about purpose much until I left for college. At age 16, I graduated from high school and decided to leave my home in Wisconsin to attend Fordham University, a liberal arts Jesuit university in New York City's Bronx neighborhood. The Jesuits lived up to their promise of educating the whole person. I was given the unique opportunity to take classes that helped expand my consciousness, and I also participated in learning experiences that went beyond the University's gates. I graduated with a degree in Urban Studies—a major I chose because it allowed me a great deal of flexibility to create an educational experience that followed my purpose and built my hustle chops. I took classes across campus that helped build my understanding of our social challenges (i.e. my Martin Luther King, Jr. and Malcolm X class) and explore cultures outside my own (my Alvin Ailey African Dance class).

My professors not only encouraged intellectual curiosity but also created a space for my hustle to thrive. When completing my senior thesis, my professor let me step outside the purely academic realm and approach the Midtown Community Court to request an internship. I convinced the Court to bring me in, and in addition to many hours of reading the work of experts, I also had the incredible experience of working with program managers, lawyers, judges, community members, law enforcement officers, and counselors who believed in providing alternatives to fines and jail as a response to low-level crimes.

While in college, I truly began my work in the service of others. I figured out how to make ends meet while learning more about my purpose. Among many odd jobs, I made money as a Red Bull representative, a resident assistant, and by teaching in the STEP program. The STEP program afforded me the opportunity to make money and stay within my purpose of shifting power dynamics. The program was designed to help underrepresented students become familiar with the same college resources—counselors, advanced classes, college fairs, application assistance—that their more privileged counterparts had.

Being the Purposeful Hustler, I also started the NYC office of LIFT, a non-profit organization that seeks to permanently eliminate poverty for families. LIFT is over 20 years old now and has successfully helped thousands of families reach their goals. In addition to founding the NYC branch of LIFT, I designed and ran a program called "Bronx and Beyond" which took children from the Fordham Bedford neighborhood on explorations throughout the city. I also ran "Young Sisters," a program for teenage girls to have a safe space to discuss what was on their mind. Even at a young age, my passion for helping others was like a fire under my feet—I could not ignore it.

Unfortunately, I often found myself frustrated by the lack of legal knowledge within many of the non-profit organizations I worked with. They didn't understand how to navigate through legal bureaucracy, and this jeopardized their programming and funding. I was also frustrated by how the law was perpetuating people's inability to break the cycle of poverty. There are policies, laws, and systems that make it unnecessarily complicated for families who are struggling. So, I did what a Purposeful Hustler does: I decided to seek knowledge that would help me be a more effective social justice advocate. After graduating from Fordham University, I eagerly enrolled at Georgetown Law, excited by the prospect of applying what I would learn to the nonprofit sector. While in law school, I continued to live in my purpose by working for the Washington, D.C. Public Defender, the Eastern District of Wisconsin Federal Defender, and by teaching in the Georgetown Street Law Program, which took me to high schools in Columbia Heights and Anacostia in Washington, D.C. The Street Law Program gave high school students power by teaching them their rights in a society that often treats them as if they don't have any.

As I had hoped, I was able to apply my new legal knowledge toward my purpose. My first job out of law school was as a staff attorney for Legal Action, a provider of free legal services to low-income individuals. Our clients came to us when they felt powerless. Most did not understand the law and did not have the financial resources to pay a private lawyer. By representing our clients, we often stood in the way of the powerful taking full advantage of them. While studying for the bar exam, I also worked tirelessly to get the Street Law Program started in Milwaukee. The experience of teaching in the Georgetown Street Law Program and working in the defender's offices prompted me to start the Street Law Program in Milwaukee at Marquette Law School. The Street Law Program takes local law students and places them around the city to teach a yearlong course in law. Most students have either no experience or have had a terrible experience with the law. They do not think about law as a source of empowerment; they fear it. However, by equipping them with knowledge about their rights, they leave the program feeling empowered. The program I started in Milwaukee has been in existence now for over 15 years and has produced amazing results.

I enjoyed my work as an adjunct professor in the Street Law Program, but I realized that it was not set up to address a fundamental underlying issue: the achievement gap in Milwaukee, which is one of the highest in the country. The achievement gap refers to the significant and persistent disparity in academic performance or educational attainment between white students and students of color. My purpose tugged at me again, and I decided to become more actively involved in reversing the trends. I have always believed that access to high-quality education is one of the most effective ways to shift power to marginalized communities. So, I set out to learn about the highest performing schools around the country and designed a school model based on what I learned. Clearly, my purpose wasn't content to be passive, living in the realm of "someday." I put some hustle in my purpose and opened up a college preparatory middle school in Milwaukee. We sought to provide our students with a high-quality education. I led the school and the Street Law Program simultaneously for five years.

After I had my first son, I decided to focus on consulting and being a new mommy. Even though I was occupied with caring for my precious little boy, my purpose still burned within me, and I became restless. This restlessness came to a head one afternoon when I decided to remove the kitchen sink and cabinets and start remodeling our kitchen by myself. After that, my husband patiently encouraged me to get out of the house!

Driven by my conviction that a lack of business acumen in the social sector was preventing organizations from realizing their full potential, I enrolled in an MBA program at the University of Wisconsin-Madison. At this point in my career, I had started numerous organizations, but I had not formally learned business principles. I wanted to test my toolbox against best practices. At the same time, I also began working for the Robert W. Baird Foundation as a Program Officer. In that role, the first of its kind at the company, I helped design the corporation's giving priorities and procedures.

Eight months pregnant with my second child and carrying a newly minted MBA, I was recruited to be the Founding CEO of the Burke Foundation, started by Trek Bikes Founder, Dick Burke. Before Dick passed away, he put all his assets into the Burke Foundation and left a relatively open mandate to spend the money primarily in Milwaukee advancing urban education and youth leadership. This role fit squarely within my purpose. The programs we supported were all about disrupting the power status quo, whether we were putting musical instruments in the hands of children who could not afford them or providing full college scholarships to young women who never dreamed college would be possible. In that role, I helped allocate millions of dollars toward the advancement of underserved youth and watched as the lives of young people around the city changed.

After helping young people bring their dreams to fruition for five years, I made yet another purpose-driven decision: I started work with a local family-owned company to explore the idea of how a corporate business could play an active role in social enterprise, beyond traditional corporate social responsibility or corporate philanthropy. In this role, I knew I could make a profound impact, and (as always) I loved the idea of marrying my career with my purpose. I operated as the President of the foundation, while simultaneously starting another company that focused on building social businesses in the health equity space. That company would ultimately become the first benefit corporation in Wisconsin, after I helped shepherd the Wisconsin Benefit Corporation legislation into existence in 2017. Benefit corporation status allows companies to include positive impact on society, workers, the community, and the environment as its legally defined goals, in addition to profit.

While in those roles, we came up with a model that would allow a corporation to be the holder of a portfolio of social enterprises that were designed to reinvest their profits toward achieving health equity—broadly defined as physical, intellectual, economic, and social equity. I also helped successfully launch a technology company, i.c. stars Milwaukee, which is focused on creating technology career paths within marginalized communities and helped lay the groundwork for the i.c. stars imprint to expand nationally.

After the benefit corporation legislation passed, and the first pilot was on its way to opening, I realized that the time was right for me to focus full-time on my own service-focused company. I leaned on my experiences and the personal toolkit I had developed to found a company that would facilitate both my hustle and my purpose. That is how Flying Elephant was born. Flying Elephant's main focus is to work with individuals, communities, and companies to create socially responsible opportunities. The company's current offerings include an imprint, Story to Tell Books, that focuses on creating children's books that feature children of color and are written and illustrated by people of color. I authored the first two books, I am a Boy of Color, and I am a Girl of Color. They are both receiving resounding enthusiasm in the marketplace from teachers, parents, and most importantly children! The other offerings of Flying Elephant include consulting, coaching, and keynote speaking. Focusing on Flying Elephant has also given me the time to write this book.

There are a couple of trends here that I think are important to note. The most important is that while my path is eclectic from a distance, a closer look reveals that there is a thread that pulls it all together. That thread is my purpose. At each step, I used my purpose to guide me. I will talk in greater detail about how I got to my purpose and how you can name yours too, but for now, take a look at the history I provided and notice that, though the work was varied, the end goal was always the same. With each career transition, I was searching for new ways to shift power to marginalized communities. All my work—opening the Bronx LIFT office, practicing law, starting the Street Law Program, administering a school, leading three foundations, starting a benefit corporation, and writing children's books—can all be traced back to that burning desire to shift power to marginalized communities.

The second important trend in my personal history is my drive to live life with a hustle. I have been able to get a lot of things done because I move in a very intentional, though not necessarily linear or traditional, way (and I'm never satisfied with working on just one project or job). My goal of leveling power dynamics has prompted me to become an "expert" in many areas and amass as much knowledge as possible to allow me to have greater impact. And when I've been unable to find suitable solutions to intrinsic challenges, I've built my own solutions.

Along the way, I've had to learn how to get over my fears, handle failure, teach myself, and take initiative on my own. Those characteristics—courage, resilience, curiosity, and initiative—are defining characteristics of the Purposeful Hustle.

Because I have been operating in this way for decades I have learned how to effectively push through challenges standing in the way of living in my purpose, and even better, how to avoid the barriers all together to create meaningful impact. This is the knowledge I hope to impart here.

What can you expect from reading this book? There are three promises I can make you. First, you will read some stories that will help carry you through the different aspects you may encounter while learning to employ a Purposeful Hustle. These stories will provide you with both caution and inspiration as you contemplate and start to activate your Purposeful Hustle. Second, each chapter includes practical techniques that you can apply on a daily basis across all aspects of your life. These techniques will guide you as you move forward. A major differentiator between this and other books is that you will be able to start to implement these techniques right away. Third, you will have the opportunity throughout this book to do actionable reflection so you can prepare to take your next steps. This time for reflection is a priceless gift. Too often we move through life withholding this gift from ourselves, but carving out time for deep reflection is crucial for the person who wants to be a Purposeful Hustler.

While there is much for you to gain from these chapters, I also have a personal motivation for writing them. This book is yet another extension of my Purposeful Hustle. You see, I believe that to shift power to marginalized people, to make real social justice change, we need to activate more people as Purposeful Hustlers. We need more people to look at our deeply entrenched social issues and feel empowered to change them. My ultimate hope is that this book will encourage you to join the positive social justice movements happening all around us and thereby leave the world a better place!

No time to waste! Let's get started!

PART ONE:

Purposeful

Finding the Force that Drives Us

CHAPTER ONE:
Purpose

Your purpose in life is to find your
purpose and give your whole heart and
soul to it.

-Gautama Buddha

Each of us has a purpose, though yours may not be crystal clear to you yet. Maybe that's why you started reading these pages. Don't worry! One of the focuses of this book is to help you clarify and articulate your purpose. Typically, clarity of purpose is not bestowed upon us in a single moment, and because of that, it can be difficult to pinpoint. Instead, it comes to us in waves throughout our lives. In order to recognize those waves, you have to put on your purpose goggles and reflect back on the moments in your life when you felt connected to something that encompassed your entire being and simultaneously felt bigger than yourself.

But what is this purpose I keep talking about and why is it so important?

Let's start with some clarity around the word purpose. The dictionary defines purpose as the reason for which something is done or created or for which something exists. When we talk about individual purpose, it means the same thing—an individual's purpose is the reason for which that person exists or was created. In my mind, purpose goes beyond personal motives (making money, getting a promotion, buying a fancy new car), and reaches outward to others, focusing on the betterment of the world. When I refer to purpose throughout this book, I am talking about this larger kind of purpose—the kind that stretches beyond the self and strives to make a positive impact.

I think about how there are billions of humans, yet each of

DEANNA SINGH

us has fingerprints that are distinct enough to be used for security purposes. I am reminded of this every time I open my cell phone with my fingerprint. I think purpose works the same way—even though there are billions of us, we each have a unique purpose. And we each have a unique imprint we can leave on the world, derived from our purpose. The question is whether or not we are going to both identify what that purpose is *and act* on it.

WHY IS PURPOSE SO IMPORTANT?

I will never forget going to a particular conference when I was about to enter my third year of law school. I had been the only student invited and was excited to attend. Before the actual conference, I was asked if I wanted to attend a pre-session with the other women attendees. I jumped at the opportunity to be around so many phenomenal women. All of them were at the top of the game—female attorneys in the general counsel's office at Fortune 500 companies. They were exceptional people who were clearly talented and successful. They even had beautiful accessories (I have never had a great fashion eye, but it was clear that many of their purses were worth more than my entire personal effects at the time!). But the questions that they were asking the moderator about health concerns, relationships, and their future were jarring. They seemed mostly miserable. As I sat there and listened to their stories, I wanted to go around and hug each of them.

When they spotted me, they made it a point to throw some of their wisdom my way:

"Don't get into the golden handcuffs."

"Don't wake up in your late 40s, wondering if you have had an impact."

"Don't wait to fulfill your purpose in life; no job or title is that important."

The scene was kind of like a "scared straight" show but with high powered attorneys and a terrified law student. I heeded their foreshadowing and started becoming much more intentional about adding time to reflect on my purpose. In my opinion, time for meaningful reflection is the thing that the women in the room were most lacking. This realization is why I schedule entire days for reflection in my calendar, why I am always doodling things about my purpose in journals, and why I have chosen to add reflection questions at the end of each chapter in this book.

WHAT ARE THE BENEFITS OF PURPOSE?

Through my reflections and lived experiences I have learned that there are many benefits of clearly defining your life's purpose. Below are a few of the most important ones:

Provides Direction: If you do not know your purpose, you may drift around without a clear sense of where your personal compass is pointing...and achieve nothing. Imagine the terror of waking up one morning and realizing that you are living someone else's life. We have all seen that movie. We can all relate to what that looks like. This is the person whose job, relationships, or life station does not align with where they want to be. The women at that conference had ambitious goals (make partner, become General Counsel, buy that beautiful car off the lot), but their goals were not tied to purpose. Their goals were tied to status, prestige, or money and, when they reached those goals, they continued to feel unfulfilled. Their experiences demonstrate why it is important for your purpose statement to extend beyond what is good for you, and include the good of other people.

What's more, when you are acting in your purpose, you will begin to see the fruits of your labor. You'll be able to connect dots and see how you are positively influencing the world around you. You'll also start to uncover even more ways to be impactful. Once you are making an impact, the opportunities continue to grow.

Builds an Innermost Circle: Many women in that conference room talked about how lonely they felt. To reach their level of success, they had neglected building relationships with significant others, family, and friends. They were struggling because when they looked around, they saw that they had accumulated a lot of wealth but had no one to share it with. And when things were dark—a grim health diagnosis, an impending layoff, a major expense—they had to weather those challenges alone because they did not have people who were part of their inner circle. Their inner circle consisted of superficial relationships tied to revenue goals, not true, heartfelt purpose.

The purposeful person knows that when they are in their purpose, it will connect them to other people who share their passions. This, in turn, allows them to develop more meaningful relationships. My friends, the people who make it into my innermost circle, are all purpose-driven people. We connected because we were attracted to that characteristic in each other.

Everyone has a different purpose, different things we are called to, but we find each other by being curious and showing up in unexpected places, by wanting to learn from other people who are changing the world and asking questions, and by boldly stating what we dream about and inviting others to join us.

Brings Peace and Joy. When you are aligned with your purpose, peace surrounds you. You begin to feel that the world is conspiring to move you forward. Even when things are in turmoil, you feel comforted. A dear friend of mine does intense work in violence prevention. What he sees on a daily basis is devastating, and I would be crippled with sadness living just one day in his role. Despite how hard the work is, he knows he is where he is supposed to be, and that his purpose is to help people navigate through their places of pain and find healing. Because he finds comfort in his purpose and peace in the middle of turmoil, he is wildly successful.

Conversely, when the women at the conference were recounting moments when they were living "the life" that they thought they wanted, they were definitely not at peace. They shared feelings of burn out, fatigue, and discontent. They were uneasy about what they were doing and how they were spending their time.

When you lay your head down at night, you will be satisfied knowing that you are in the space you were meant to occupy. You'll find joy in getting up to do the work, talking about your work, and bringing other people into the work. You'll find joy in your successes.

HOW IS YOUR PURPOSE REVEALED?

Let me share one of the most poignant memories of one of the many times when my purpose revealed itself to me.

It was 5:00 a.m. I had barely slept the night before. I don't think my parents slept either. We all got up, got dressed, and went out to the minivan. My father was not going with us, but he was standing in the driveway asking questions, stalling. He asked my mother:

"Do you have the directions?" She was prone to get into the car and drive without a particular destination, so that was a fair question.

"Did you pack her some medicine?" Boy, did she pack me medicine! I could have opened my own little pharmacy with all the medicine she packed me. For the next four years, my friends would sometimes refer to my dorm room as Walgreens.

"Are you sure you have everything?"

I was the first in the family to go to college. We had no idea what "going to college" meant except that if I went there, I would be on the "right" pathway. To my parents, college meant security; college meant that all their sacrifices were paying off. Since we didn't know what going to college entailed, we had packed *everything*. I wish we had been working off a "here are some appropriate things to bring to college" list. But we were not.

In addition to the small pharmacy, I had a three-pronged gold floor lamp that we had purchased from the bootleg furniture store. I had an electric can opener, tea kettle, microwave, and burners. Perhaps the strangest thing I had was a box of white china. My mother had found it at a rummage sale. I was pretty sure I didn't need to bring my china to college, but she had insisted, "Maybe you will want to have a fancy dinner." I would travel with those plates in the same box for ten years, to 25+ locations. I would never open them until I was married. If you come to my house now for dinner, you will likely eat off those plates because I plan to get every inch of use out of them possible.

I had been in a hurry to leave home. I graduated at age 16, not because of some crazy intelligence, but because I was anxious to be on my own. To achieve early graduation, I had taken the maximum number of classes, even going to school an hour early for what we called "0 hour," to gain an extra class hour in addition to the regular periods. I also maxed out the core classes I could take in all subjects, except math.

I enjoyed high school for the most part, but my father was strict. I was expected to either be at school, home, or with my family. Things like sleepovers and dances were not part of my high school experience. College was a way to spread my wings.

I chose to go to Fordham University in the Bronx, NYC for school. Why? Namely, because of that Frank Sinatra song, "If I can make it there, I'll make it anywhere." Now that I have children of my own, I realize how challenging it must have been for my parents to send me so far away at such a young age. The Bronx and a small Wisconsin suburb share few similarities.

My father must have been keenly aware of the differences between our home and NYC because he sat me down one day and told me to get out a piece of paper. He then began to dictate a list of rules for college. Here is a sampling of some of his expectations:

- You will never leave campus without a chaperone
- You will always keep your room clean
- You will not talk to any boys—only girls, and your teachers
- You will call home at least one time every day

He was serious about his list. He even asked me to get it notarized! (I didn't).

We all stood in the driveway the morning of my departure for a long time. Silence. No one knew what to say. Awkwardly, my father reached out to hug me, and I lost it. What the heck was I doing? Why would I ever want to leave those arms that had protected me so well?

He patted me heartily on the back. "Okay, okay," he said in his Indian accent, signaling to me that the crying needed to stop. But when I pulled away from him, I could see that he had tears welling in his eyes too. I had only seen my father teary-eyed a few times in my life. My crying multiplied as our packed-to-the-brim teal minivan pulled away. I remember him walking behind the car, hands behind his back, watching us pull out of the driveway. He kept walking behind us until I couldn't see him anymore.

We then went to pick up my grandmother, affectionately called Big Mama. Though she was only about 110 pounds and 4'10", she had a BIG personality. By this time, it was 5:30 a.m. and Big Mama was sitting on her front porch, surrounded by people from up and down the block. The street looked more like a block party than the crack of dawn. It took me a minute to realize this was for me. Big Mama had told everyone on the block that I was going to college, and they had woken up early to see me off!

The kids I had played with my whole life came up and told me, half smiling, to not forget them. The other grandmothers on the street gave me cake wrapped in foil for the voyage and big warm hugs. The aunts and uncles that lived in my grandmother's house beamed at me and told me how proud they were.

Though my mother and Big Mama were traveling for only three

or four days, Big Mama had multiple suitcases, and a stack of hat boxes at her side with some of her beautiful Sunday Crowns neatly tucked away. When I asked what she was doing with all that stuff, she told me matter-of-factly, "I have never been to college before; I didn't know what to wear."

When I thought about all of those people—my mom with the china and medications, the neighbors on the block with their good wishes and baked goods, my grandmother with her hats, my teary-eyed father—I understood the privilege I had been given.

As we headed east, my thoughts wandered back to my grandmother's street. No one else on the block was going to college that year, even though plenty of them were of college-going age. In my family, none of my aunts and uncles had gone to college, let alone my parents. I was the one—the one everyone was putting their hope in. I was the horse they had bet on. They had all paid for me to be there, in that minivan, about to start a new adventure. I had worked hard, but I had not "earned" my privilege. My privilege had been fought for and won by the people who were sending me on my way. I was lucky. My parents figured out how to bend their life trajectories to get a piece of the "power pie," and they gave it to me. The people who had been part of my sendoff, through no fault of their own, were not so lucky. They did not have access to the same power. They were, because of systemic barriers, left on the margins of society, unable to get the kind of jobs, education, homes, medical treatment, and social securities that the powerful take for granted. I found that imbalance unacceptable, and it became clear to me that my future steps would carry me toward the goal of dismantling those systemic barriers.

With my purpose beginning to crystallize, I walked onto that college campus and decided to bring all the people who had helped me. I was the first to go to college, but I was determined to NOT be the last. I decided to make this opportunity, and the subsequent ones that opened up for me, a chance to pay homage to all those who let me stand on their shoulders. Who, through their sacrifices, helped me kick open doors. I decided early on that my purpose in life would be forever entangled in all of them—my family, my community. The people who worked day-in, day-out, but struggled to get ahead due to the biased systems of power that gave them an innate disadvantage.

This calling spoke to me. And I answered.

The story of my first day of college, and the other stories that occupy the pages of this book, will not only illustrate triumphs and challenges from my personal journey, but will also provide lessons and actionable advice that can be applied to your own Purposeful Hustle. In subsequent chapters, we will talk about how to clarify your purpose, and how to use it to push past fear, make decisions, positively impact the world, and fuel your "change the world" hustle!

ACTIVE REFLECTION:

Before we go any further, I'd like you to stop here and think about the idea of purpose. No need to write a personal purpose statement now; instead, reflect on the importance of purpose and how comfortable you feel with the idea of placing your purpose at the center of your life. In the next chapter, we will walk through a three-step practice that will make your purpose tangible, but this first reflection opportunity will give you a baseline for thinking about personal purpose.

1. How do you feel about the word purpose?

2. How do you feel about the idea that everyone has a purpose in life?

3. If someone close to you was asked what your purpose is, would they be able to answer accurately based on how you live your life? In other words, are you living your life in alignment with your purpose?

CHAPTER TWO:
Find and Test Your Purpose

There is no greater gift you can give
or receive than to honor your calling.
It is why you were born and how you
become most truly alive.

-Oprah Winfrey

A t a young age, I had this *sense* that I wanted to be part of something bigger than myself. That sense showed up for me most predominantly in culminating moments, like the one I described in the introduction about the day I left for college. When we drove away from grandmother's house that morning, I reflected on all of the people who had paved the way for my new world of opportunity. Deep within me, I felt a sense of responsibility, a calling to work hard to make sure I multiplied the gift I had been given and passed it on to others.

We all have senses that we rely on to make decisions, choose different paths, and weigh options. My purpose started as a vague feeling, and it took some uncomfortable situations (which I describe later in this chapter) to help me realize that I needed to do a better job of naming that inner sense. Purpose is a way to name that inner feeling. It is a vehicle that brings together those senses into something cohesive. Four techniques—reflection, writing, testing, and iteration—have helped me refine my purpose into what it is today, an invaluable tool that I use every day of my life. I have been able to see how incredibly powerful it is to be able to name your purpose and live your life based on it. If you follow these four techniques (I address them in more detail later in this chapter), I am confident you will be well on your way to naming your purpose.

THE CONSEQUENCES OF NOT NAMING YOUR PURPOSE

I realized the power of having a clearly defined purpose

DEANNA SINGH

by seeing how not having one jeopardized my ability to make a meaningful impact in the world. There are two moments when the consequences of not having a solid stated purpose became glaringly obvious to me...

I sat across from a priest. I could tell he was perplexed. He was the most senior person on the search committee of an organization that was recruiting me to take on a leadership position. He had a few pieces of paper in front of him, one of which was the results of a test I had taken meant to identify interests and talents. He was perplexed because I had high scores in all four of the testing categories. Usually, people only showed one or two areas of interest, and that helped the hiring team determine whether or not the person would fit the role. I think this methodology has flaws, but that is a topic for another conversation. Here is how my conversation with the priest went:

"Deanna, you meet all the qualifications we are looking for; in fact, you actually fit the qualifications for multiple roles, not just this one."

I responded graciously, "Thank you." I was confused though because while his words were complimentary, his tone was not.

He went on: "However, the fact that you are showing up all over the radar on this test, and the fact that you have such varied experiences actually makes it harder to pinpoint whether or not you would be good in this role."

I felt myself get defensive and tried to explain that, while I had done many different things throughout my career, all of it was motivated by my purpose. I probably bumbled through a variety of words, trying to articulate my personal purpose and how it continued to play a role in my career. I knew what I meant and I figured that he would understand too, especially given his profession. I was wrong.

Later that week, after progressing to the final round, the priest called me to let me know that I did not get the position. The other candidate, who had been doing the same thing for two decades and only scored high in one quadrant, had more "focus" than I did, and they felt more comfortable offering him the position. I put the word focus in quotes because I think they mischaracterized me. It was not that I did not have focus, my problem was that I could not articulate my focus well to others and that came across during the interview process. My focus was different than the other candidate who was focused on a singular occupation, a job. My focus was on living out my purpose. I am glad I didn't get the job because that interaction with the company exhibited a lack of creativity. Not my kind of environment! However, I gained a valuable lesson from the experience. I realized that if I didn't help people understand what moved me, they could easily come to their own inaccurate conclusions. It became imperative for me to name my purpose, not just for myself, but for other people.

I needed to help others understand how my story fit together and trying to express a "sense" was not going to cut it.

The inability to articulate my purpose has had personal consequences too. I am able to handle an inordinate number of moving pieces at one time and can be deeply involved across a spectrum of projects while staying fully engaged with all of them. But my ability to move between differing things is not boundless, and I learned this the hard way.

Early in my career, I was doing a lot of things, but nothing particularly well. I will not, for the sake of ink, list out all my activities and commitments at the time, but suffice it to say, I had less than six hours of rest time, including sleep, scheduled into my day.

How did I get myself into such a predicament? I thought the game was about quantity. If I said yes to everything, that was the best way to live out my purpose, right? Wrong. In my willingness to say yes to everything, I drifted away from my purpose and started doing things I *could* do. I mistakenly thought that if I could do something, especially if I could do it well, I was *supposed* to do it. I was going to meetings where I could offer or gain very little, attending random events, and working on projects that were outside of my scope. Why? Because I thought that no one would ask me to do things I shouldn't be doing. Boy, was I wrong. People will ask you to do all kinds of things. Without a purpose filter on, you will find yourself headed down a path that was not meant for you.

I share these stories because each of them reflects how important it is to move from having a general sense of purpose to one that is fully articulated. In the first instance, I knew how I was living my purpose, but not what my purpose statement was, so I was unable to help the interviewer understand how the pieces of my life snapped together. In the second instance, because I was not using my purpose to make decisions, I ended up in a hole that was hard to dig myself out of. The question you should ask yourself is: How do I avoid ending up in these situations? The answer is rooted in being able to find clarity in your purpose.

> It became imperative for me to name my PURPOSE, not just for myself, but for other people.

BRING YOUR PURPOSE INTO FOCUS

Perhaps you are thinking that this business about living in your purpose sounds great in theory, but you have no idea what your purpose is. To know what your purpose is, you have to create some time to work on it. Think of your purpose as a road stretching out in front of you. How can you traverse the road if your windows are fogged up and you can't see the path clearly? You need to take time to defog the glass and gain clarity of purpose. How?

Though I am not a philosopher, I have read enough philosophy to know that it is likely impossible to get to a definite answer about who you are and what your absolute purpose may be. However, pursuing the question, particularly about how you want to impact the world, is a wise and worthy exercise that can help give you a stronger direction in life. The good news is that even if you haven't spent a lot of time reflecting on your purpose, you likely already have an inclination about what it is. Four steps—reflection, writing, testing, and iteration—will help you gain even greater clarity. The following sections are broken down into these four categories. I will show you how these steps have played out for me, and then offer some techniques for you to incorporate them into your own life.

REFLECTION

To figure out what my purpose was, I had to do a lot of reflection. Reflection is critical for the person who wants to be a Purposeful Hustler. The Purposeful Hustler knows that if they don't stay vigilant about who they are, how they are showing up in the world, and what impact they are or aren't making, they cannot be on top of their game. They recognize that it is in the moments of reflection that they can piece things together to either build on their success or learn from their failures Too often we are on the treadmill of life and do not give ourselves this free and precious gift. Of all the skills a Purposeful Hustler must have, reflection is critical. You cannot gain clarity of purpose without (1) making time for reflection and (2) asking the right questions.

One practice I would highly encourage is setting aside a full day to reflect on purpose. Setting aside a day, especially the first time you reflect on purpose, is critical. In the next section, you will be given a series of questions that require you to process a lot of emotions and thoughts. Having unrushed time will afford you the opportunity to process those emotions and thoughts thoroughly.

I have made full-day reflection an annual tradition. I used to fret about taking a whole day and worried that it was inefficient. However, I have learned that quite the opposite is true. Dedicating a full day to reflection gives me the time to really go deep into my thoughts. I look forward to my annual day of reflection because it is a time for me to learn, celebrate my accomplishments, and look ahead to what might be next. During this day, I review my purpose statement and ask myself the hard questions that get lost in the day-to-day. It's an effective way for me to make sure I am creating time to regularly focus on purpose and push myself to take meaningful actions.

In addition to your full day of reflection, it's crucial to make time in your daily life for reflection. There are a lot of different options to consider for ways to insert daily contemplation into your life. To get you thinking about your options, let's take a look at some of the methods I have tested and what I've learned from each:

Meditation. I envy people who are able to reflect through meditation. I would love to meditate, but I am really bad at it. I have,

> " **Of all the skills a Purposeful Hustler must have, reflection is critical.** "

as they say in the meditating world, a very active "monkey brain." It is hard for me to stop thinking about a million different things at once. I have had different times in my life when I was able to spend more time practicing meditation and I witnessed a notable difference. I felt calmer and better able to stay focused for longer periods of times. Though I am not there yet, I am an aspiring meditator.

Daily Journaling. I love this idea, and I believe in it. But again, I am not very good at it. However, I do write a LOT of things down, and I am sure that I write down things every day that pertain to my goals. It's just not in one place! I take notes across many different platforms, my computer, my phone, and whatever random journal is at my fingertips. I am working hard to use only one repository because daily journaling is an aspirational goal for me, but even my random assortment of notes have been incredibly valuable. I am able to review them and double check that I am staying on course with my purpose.

Talking it Out. I LOVE this strategy (but have to be careful not to abuse it!). When I know I am in the mood to talk out my thoughts, I try to be respectful and preface the conversation with my would-be listener with warnings like, "I am wondering if I can take ten minutes of your time to flesh out some things I have been thinking about and get your opinion," or "I have some questions about how I am living out my purpose and I am wondering if I can share them with you. I would appreciate being able to talk it out."

I find that it is really valuable to share what I am thinking, questioning, and feeling with people I trust. I appreciate being able to hear their perspectives, and their responses help me gain greater clarity.

Get Physical. Some of my very best revelations come when I am engaging my body physically, and not necessarily mentally. When I have a big decision coming up, or I need to regain clarity, I go for a run. I run on treadmills and will often stop to jot down thoughts that come to me. I find that being physical lets my mind and body work together toward solutions.

Sometimes I will focus on one aspect of my purpose during the entire workout. I like doing this because it allows me to concentrate on specific things, and lets my thoughts bubble around a central topic as I work out.

Prayer. Praying helps me stay grounded in my purpose. Practicing my faith has always been important to me, and I have found prayer to be an appealing reflective tool for many reasons. I don't have to still my brain; I can let it go wherever it wants. I can also pray anywhere and at any time. I can pray when I am lying still or when I am moving about in my day. I tend to pray all day, daily—I start when my alarm goes off in the morning, spending the first fifteen minutes in prayer, and pray at the end of the day, right before I sleep. I also pray in a conversational manner, so it feels more comfortable and accessible.

After finding the time to reflect, the next obvious question is: What does the Purposeful Hustler reflect on?

If you spend your time reflecting on what reality tv show you watched last night, it is likely not going to bring you any closer to your purpose. When you are reflecting with the intention of clarifying your purpose, try to answer these two primary questions: (1) What are your passions? and (2) How have your experiences uniquely positioned you for impact?

When I took the time to really reflect on these two questions, I found that I am most passionate about disrupting systems of power in favor of those who are often marginalized. How did I get there? I realized that my most overwhelming moments occur when I am able to help someone else break down traditional power dynamics. My passion is ignited during transformational moments, like when an underrepresented student finds out they are getting a full scholarship, when the social entrepreneur gets their first client, when the mentee quits her job to pursue her calling, when an organization meets their social mission, when a mother opens her first savings account, or when a family buys their first home. These are the moments I live for. In each of these instances, an important thing is taking place: Each one of these people and organizations are realizing a new level of power. That is highly motivating to me.

I also realized that I have been consistently drawn into helping marginalized communities. I care deeply about equity and have intentionally focused on working within communities that are often left on the periphery. Amongst others, I have worked alongside seniors, immigrants, people of color, children, the economically distressed, and incarcerated people. I believe passionately that when all of us are able to realize our potential, we will all truly be free.

How am I uniquely positioned for impact? To answer this second reflection question, I looked closely at my experiences, knowledge, and skills. Each of those assets are the direct result of my unique position in the world.

My parents have been deeply influential in my life. They have given me many gifts, but one of the greatest was that they raised me in a multicultural home. That experience has allowed me to hone some of the most important tools in my toolkit. I have the ability to build bridges between different groups because I was constantly helping different people understand each other by translating language and culture. I can easily move from one space to another (my husband calls this moving from the boardroom to the block, because I spent equal amounts of my time between the suburbs and the city).

Another skill in my toolkit that helps position me for impact is empathy. Over time, my empathy has deepened as I've witnessed how different people live and why.

As I reflected, I came to understand how these characteristics— the ability to build bridges, move fluidly between spaces, and be empathetic—are a critical part of my purpose. When I saw those experiences, knowledge, and skills together, I recognized that I am uniquely equipped to understand people of various backgrounds and positions of power, move between the players, and help them reach common ground. In short, my reflection showed me that I could use my unique set of skills and experiences to activate my purpose and disrupt traditional power dynamics.

YOUR TURN: NAME YOUR PASSION

Let's see if we can get closer to identifying YOUR purpose by walking through this process.

First, what technique will you use for reflection? How much time can you set aside? How will you commit to incorporating regular reflection into your life? As listed above, there are many methods for reflection, but no matter which you use, I highly suggest starting with a FULL day of reflection.

You might find a full day of reflection to be impactful because it's a time you can intentionally plan around. For me, working full-time and having a young family requires a pretty tight calendar. If something is going to get done, I put it on the calendar. If I see that it is coming, I can make sure to deliberately carve out time and turn my thoughts toward it. I typically do this annual retreat in late fall in anticipation of the New Year, but you don't have to wait! Schedule it whenever you are ready. If you are thinking about what is going to work best for you, consider the nuances present in your life right now. Can you afford to take a full day? Do you already have time set aside that you could use for reflection? Are you going on a vacation soon? Do you have a work holiday coming up that you could take advantage of?

In addition to a full day, it is important to set up daily reflection practices. Are you already building in time to reflect, but perhaps without intentionally thinking about your purpose? Which reflection techniques might fit your lifestyle? How can you embrace some of these daily reflection rituals before your big reflection day?

You may not be worried about the time, but rather what you are going to do with the time. Which brings us to the next question: Once you have the time set aside, what will you reflect on? Try applying the same two questions I posed earlier: (1) What is your passion? and (2) How have your experiences uniquely positioned you for impact?

Explore Your Passions

"What are you passionate about?" This is one of my favorite questions to ask total strangers. No one ever expects it. I ask this because it allows me to learn exciting things about people. Sometimes, maybe out of habit, the person to whom I ask the question will just give me their title and organization's name. When this happens, I just ask them again. After they get over the initial shock of the question, they almost always come back with something pretty impressive.

And while the people sitting next to me are chatting about the weather, we are talking about turtles going extinct, the painting they are working on, or the organization for which they volunteer their time. I learn so much from this one simple question. I also ask this question because I have come to realize that society doesn't make it easy for people to talk about the things they are most passionate about. I love watching people's shoulders release tension, and their eyes light up as they share what brings them joy and stirs their hearts.

This is the very first question a would-be Purposeful Hustler must answer for themselves: What are YOU most passionate about? Why are you excited about that issue? What pulls you into it? Grounding yourself in a deep understanding of your passions is a critical first step. So, how does one figure out what they are most passionate about? Don't worry; it is not going to be hard to find out, and you may already know.

The thing about passions is that we are often taught to bury them, to push them to the backburner, when we make a decision. We are taught to relegate them to buckets like "maybe when I retire," or "if I can just get more stable in my career/family/etc." Or we are taught not to mix our passion with our work. Passion is what we do when we are not working; they can't be the same thing. I am living proof that these statements are fallacies. It *is* possible to put your passion at the center of your life—I've seen it happen time and again in both my life and the lives of others.

PASSION is often
masked as a luxury
when it is really
an essential
ingredient in life.

If you are still struggling to name your passions, try this trick. Take a close look at your behaviors. Why? Because, in my experience, passions are often revealed through behavior. Here are a few behaviors to observe that might help you discover or rediscover your passions:

- What do you like doing? Is there an activity that you could do for hours and not realize how much time has passed? How do you currently spend your free time? If you did not have to work for money, what would you want to dedicate your time to?

- What topic is always on the tip of your tongue? What kinds of conversations energize you? What do you never grow tired of talking about? What problem would you like to be a part of solving? If you could influence just one thing, what would it be?

- What do you think about constantly? Is there a topic area you're especially interested in? What consumes your thoughts if you let it? What do you read, research, or try to earn about without any other prompting? Is there any social issue that has kept you up at night in the past year?

- What brings you joy? Are there situations in which you feel pure happiness or something close to it?

- Who do you look up to? Why?

- What do you want to be remembered for when you die?

- What are the times in your life when you have felt the most productive? The most engaged? What was similar about those times? Are there any common themes?

Maybe none of these questions are sparking ideas because you don't have a current life situation that allows you to pursue your passions. If that is the case, think about the list of questions through the lens of IF. If you could live in a space where your passions were thriving, how would you answer these questions?

One of the significant challenges that may arise when you explore your passions is the realization that you are passionate about a lot of different things. I recently talked to a young man who told me he wanted to make sure he was using his spare time and resources to positively impact the community around him. His goal was ambitious, but he was having a hard time getting started because he did not know *where to* start. When I asked him what he was passionate about, he listed: access to higher education, technology, and water. These are three seemingly disparate areas of passion, and under them, there are many different issues. So, I started to drill him with a list of additional questions.

My line of questioning was simple. What do you mean when you say those words higher education, technology, and water? What does access to higher education mean to you? Why is it important? He shared that he wanted to see more people of color accessing high-quality education because this was such a game changer in his life.

Then, I asked him why technology was important to him. He explained that, in his mind, technology was a tool that could bring greater equality, as it allowed people of all backgrounds to be in a field with significant opportunity for upward financial mobility.

And finally, water? He explained that he was deeply concerned about how flippant we are with our water resources and wished more people were actively engaged in protecting water, since many people across the globe are struggling with little or low-quality water.

In about 30 minutes, we figured out a plan to incorporate all three of his passions. Initially, he thought that his areas of interests were so different that he needed to choose one and put his focus on it. But as we talked more, he realized he could pull together all three. He understood that if he could help create a pipeline of underrepresented people into colleges and programs that focus on water technology fields, he would be hitting all three of his passions. More importantly, he realized that being passionate about three seemingly disparate things did not distance him from identifying his purpose—it actually made it easier to see. What cut across all three of those passions was the idea of creating equal access. He could see that he had ONE singular purpose—equal access—and he was specifically interested in seeing that purpose applied to higher education, technology, and water.

Being able to go through the exercise of naming his passions and then stepping back to see the familiar threads—the purpose that was tying everything together—allowed him to walk out of my office with greater clarity on how to focus his energy.

It will not always work out this way. You may have passions that do not fit into your purpose. That is okay. Your job is not to squash those passions, but to recognize them for what they are: passions that are not central to your purpose. You can still pursue them, and I would argue that you should, but they cannot occupy your primary attention because they are peripheral passions, not central to your purpose.

MATCHING PASSION WITH TALENTS & EXPERIENCES

Now let's get a little more specific and tackle the second reflection question: How have your experiences uniquely positioned you for impact? Explore how you can leverage your background to make a difference in your purpose area. Sometimes this is hard to see because it might be right in front of your face!

Here are some questions that might help you identify what you are uniquely positioned to do:

- Are there any unique experiences in your life—either good or bad—that have had a major impression on you?

- Do you have a unique skill set? This does not have to be something you are professionally trained in, but it could be. Are you great at problem-solving? Bringing unique groups together? Artistic expression? Writing?

- Is there something that comes easily to you, but others struggle with it?

- What are you routinely asked to advise on? Do people call you frequently when they are having a particular issue?

- Is there anything that you would be considered an expert in?

- Do you have unique knowledge? For example, can you read, write, or speak in a different language? Do you have a background in agriculture? Are you highly versed in technology?

As I mentioned, it might be hard to identify what you are uniquely positioned to do at first. You may have to take some time to really explore what it means to you. You might have to enlist the help of some people who are familiar with you and will be honest. You could ask them the same questions from above. If they know you, they will be able to help you list a few of the things that are unique to you!

TAPPING INTO YOUR ROOTS

Here is a hack, a way for you to get closer to your unique value proposition. A value proposition is what distinguishes you from others. Think about your origin story. This does not have to mean your childhood story. I am referring to a time when you started to "sense" a purpose bigger than yourself.

For some people, their origin story is rooted in their personal history. Some people's history allows them to see the value of the work they are doing. Either they had a really positive experience—one that shaped their lives and motivated them to share similar experiences with others—or they had a negative one, and they want to spread the resources that helped them overcome it, or attempt to remedy the injustice. There are also people who come to this work because of their studies. Through learning experiences, travel, reading, or becoming acquainted with someone outside of their network, they gain a better understanding of what is happening in the world and, though not directly impacted by the injustices, want to be involved in a solution. One way is not better than the other. They both require a critical mindset.

Another common origin story revolves around something specific that has happened to you. When I think about the young people who are stepping into the social justice limelight because they were personally impacted by gun violence, I see a perfect example of how a circumstance can reveal a greater purpose in your life. This is common when a person has gone through something extreme, either bad or good. A parent who takes up gun issues after losing a child in a school shooting or a person who fights for equal access to non-traditional medicine after being healed are both examples of how these moments can reveal one's purpose.

Reflect on your personal history or origin story. Did you experience a pivotal moment that may help define your life's purpose? What brought you to that moment? What was happening when you felt like you wanted to become more engaged? Your experiences can have a powerful influence on your core purpose.

Recently, a young man shared that after doing some reflection he realized he was most driven by helping people combat stereotypes that often accompany mental health issues, particularly in the African American community. His father struggled with mental health issues, and as a child he never felt he had all the resources to understand and help him. He sensed how wrong it was that people did not want to talk to him about what was going on because of the attached stigma. This made him confused and vulnerable. Reflecting on his experience helped him to see that he has a perspective many others in the field do not. Recognizing his unique position helped him gain greater clarity of purpose and allowed him to see how he, as an individual, could activate change. That was a significant step for him, and now, with his greater clarity, he is having a major impact in the area he is most passionate about. He has connected dots he would have been blind to had he not spent time in intentional reflection.

Reflection is a great exercise, even for those who feel like they already know their purpose. Everyone is guilty of not reflecting enough, even though it's helpful for coping with change, making major decisions, or digesting new information or circumstances. It is a good idea to reflect often because your life situation may change from one month to the next—or even one day to the next!

After I had a sense of my passions and unique value proposition, it was time to write a draft of my purpose statement. At the beginning of this chapter, I shared how I struggled to articulate my purpose statement to myself and others, and the consequences of not being able to do that. I recognized how much I needed clarity around my purpose and was motivated to write it out. Freewriting my thoughts helped me brainstorm and concretize my purpose into a statement. This also made it possible to memorize it. After engaging in deep reflection, the second step is to write your purpose statement.

The most important thing I did during this step was force myself to write out ALL the ways I had been defining my purpose. This was a brain dump of all of the things that I used to say when talking about my purpose throughout the years. My list looked something like this:

"My purpose is...

...to multiply my skills, experiences, and opportunities for others."

...to be a voice for the voiceless."

...to help others to reach their full potential."

...to disrupt power."

...to empower others to be their best."

After I wrote down all the things that came to mind, I started looking for themes and quickly noticed repetition. Just seeing them on paper helped me see the underlying themes. I could see that I am about creating change, challenging the status quo, and serving alongside others.

Next, I spent time dissecting the words. Words matter, so I forced myself to pay close attention to all the words I was using. The words that stood out to me included power, potential, and others. I realized that there were some words that did not really make sense. I love the word empower, but empowerment is in the hands of the individual. I cannot empower someone, only they can empower themselves. When I dissected the words, I realized what I really wanted was to shift power. That distinction has become important to me because I try to stay focused on activities that allow individuals to OWN their power, not rely on others.

Last, I pushed myself to come up with one sentence that summarized my purpose in life, could be shared with others, and could be committed to memory. What is the point of having a purpose statement if it is incomprehensible or too long? Committing to memory may seem like an odd requirement but this is also wildly important. It is very useful to be able to remember your purpose because when you do, it becomes easier to actually call it up when you need it.

Try it now! If you had to write out your purpose statement, what would it say? Don't stress out! This does not need to be complicated. In fact, the simpler, the better. Start with, "My purpose is..." and go from there. You can refine it as you learn more and gain more clarity. Right now, let this be a starting point and be open to how it might evolve!

Naming Your Purpose

I am passionate about. . .	I am uniquely positioned to. . .

My (DRAFT) Purpose is. . .

Moving your thoughts from your brain to the paper is an essential step in the reflection process. This will allow you to take something that can be amorphous and make it tangible. If you write down a purpose statement and you feel it is not perfect, that's okay. In addition to time and just letting it sit with you a while, the next few exercises will help you scrub down the purpose statement even further.

Why does this matter? Because living a life of purpose and trying to change the world is not easy. Social change work is personal. Social change work will challenge you at your very core. If you are unclear about why you are in the work, you will be shaken, and it will be hard to recover. The purpose statement will be an essential compass for you.

TEST YOUR PURPOSE!

Testing your purpose might seem scary at first, but there is real value to it. The only way to know whether or not you have picked the right purpose statement is to test it. There are a lot of mission statements, strategic plans, and vision boards that have no practical application beyond collecting dust. A purpose statement that is not actively tested is just as useless.

Let the purpose statement you've written be a useful tool. Let it guide your commitments and decision-making. There is not a day that goes by that I do not use my purpose statement to make a decision. This statement helps me open and close doors. It helps me articulate to others who I am and what I believe. When I am unclear about where and how I should be spending my time, my purpose statement allows me to get refocused. Your purpose statement can help you in those same ways too if you let it.

Here are a few ways to test your purpose statement:
1. Intuitive Check
2. Support Network Check
3. Calendar Check
4. Decision Check

When I was in law school, the way I articulated my purpose was to "use my blessings, opportunities, and experiences to impact the lives of others." When I tested this purpose statement, it worked. The first three tests on the list were pretty easy. It intuitively felt right and seemed in alignment with my purpose. I felt the most joy when I was doing things in school, like teaching children in local high schools, serving in leadership positions to help increase the number of people of color in higher education, and fighting for equal rights for immigrants.

The second test, talking to my family and friends, was straightforward too. Many people knew how much I loved working in community-related projects that directly impacted the lives of others. My friends knew that if they wanted me to get excited about something, there had to be a multiplying community effect. Meaning I was not going to get up at 5:00 a.m. to go workout unless we first served in a breakfast program for homeless individuals.

The third test involves comparing your calendar with your purpose statement. With a written purpose statement, I went through the list of all the things I was doing in my life. I literally started recording what I did every day and how much of it, on a percentage basis, was spent in purpose-related activities. I added up the hours that I was awake and divided that by how much of it was "in my purpose." This exercise helped me see that the majority of my activities were aligned with my purpose. Outside of school and work, almost all my free time was spent doing things that supported my goal of impacting lives, such as volunteering or teaching. It has certainly become harder to closely track my calendar as I have gotten older but doing so helps keep a semblance of harmony.

The last test, running a major decision through my purpose, was more challenging than the other checks, but it was the most important...

When it came time for graduation from law school, I remember sitting on the floor of the Street Law Program office. I had a few offers in front of me. All of them were things I was interested in. All of them had potential. One of the offers—a position in NYC— came with a paycheck with a great deal of zeroes in it. Another was for a job in D.C. with a fantastic title. The third was for a job in Milwaukee, working for Legal Action of Wisconsin as a staff attorney in the senior law division, and it offered less money than what I was making in my odds and ends jobs during law school.

I was very unsettled about the decision. I called a bunch of people in my inner circle, perplexed about what to do. Did I go for the money and big city? The title and proximity to power? Or the job in my hometown working for people who could not afford legal counsel?

It may seem odd that the third one was on the list—it certainly did to those people who were looking at it through the lens of money, prestige, and location. They were adamant that I should take one of the first two options and had logical reasons for their selections. There are more opportunities in NYC and D.C.; my adult friend base was in those two cities; I had created meaningful relationships in those cities; the jobs had a clear pathway for me to ascend to other coveted positions; and the paychecks would be a nice boost as I went into the real world.

I love the network of people I have gathered over the years as advisors. They are wiser than I am, and I depend on them a lot. In most instances, their opinions weigh heavily into my decisions and yet, as I sat on that floor, their advice was not resonating with me at all. So I pulled out my purpose statement and inspected each one of the offers through that lens. What job would have the greatest impact on the lives of others? What would further my purpose? The clear winner was Legal Action of Wisconsin. I took the least glamorous, smallest city with the lowest paying job offer, and the minute I decided to do so, I felt at peace. I am confident I could have done well in the other positions, but they simply didn't align with my purpose as closely as the Milwaukee job did. I told my advisors my decision and shared with them that, while enticing, the NYC/D.C. positions would have kept me in really tall, beautifully furnished buildings, but not in proximity with the communities I felt destined to serve. They all understood. They know how important purpose is to me and how intentional I am about following it. Now, before they give me any advice, they always start with questions about purpose alignment.

I have often encountered similar intersections in my career. Companies have put offers on the table that made my head spin, but at each pivotal moment, I have come back to the question of purpose and let that be the primary deciding factor. Purpose has not held me back. In fact, it has accelerated my work. I have been able to move through many sectors, leapfrog into leadership experience as a CEO, Executive Director, and President all before the age of 35, and realize my purpose over and over again. Despite how enticing the title and pay may be, I have consistently chased purpose. I have no regrets. It has not failed me. Those four tests—the Intuitive Check, Support Network Check, Calendar Check, and Decision Check—continue to help me test and refine my purpose statement.

YOUR TURN: TEST YOUR PURPOSE STATEMENT

It is time to apply the tests to your purpose statement. Using the draft statement of your purpose, first test whether or not it intuitively feels right. This is totally appropriate because in many ways the purpose statement should be a verbal manifestation of your innermost desires. Can you memorize it? If you need to recall your purpose within seconds, could you? Does it make you smile? Does it *feel* right?

At the beginning of the book we talked about how knowing your purpose should achieve the following:

- Provides direction
- Builds an innermost circle
- Brings you peace and joy

Of course, you will not know the full answers to these questions until you put your purpose into action, but you can take an educated guess about them. When you look at your purpose statement, do you think it will help you determine what is next? By pursuing it, will you likely be able to build your network of people who share your values and convictions? Does your purpose statement bring you a feeling of deep satisfaction?

The next test point involves the people you love. Make a list of the people who know you best, your secret keepers. Also, add people to your list who inspire you—those who you feel have made it or are doing what you want to be doing. Ask the people on your list: "Given what you know about the world, and me, do you think that this purpose statement makes sense?" You could go further and ask them: "How do you think I could live out that purpose in a meaningful way?" You will likely learn a lot from their feedback.

After you talk to your loved ones and those who inspire you, it is time to check your current schedule against your purpose statement. How much of your time is being spent on purpose-related activities? The results might not be great at first. The data could be scary, illuminating, or depressing. There certainly have been times when I did the exercise and felt that way.

Today, I don't go through the full extent of the exercise. My shorthand way of doing the same thing is thinking about this scenario: If I were followed around by a reality TV crew, would they be able to identify my purpose? If I told them my purpose, would they call me a liar? Just that little mental game helps me keep myself in check.

If the results of your calendar calculations are not good, you may have to go through the painful process of removing yourself from projects that just don't align with your purpose. This has happened to me on more than one occasion. I was honest with people and just said, "Your project is still important to me, but I have to curb my involvement in order to stay focused on the things that align more directly with my purpose." I still struggle with this, because I like to say yes to interesting projects and people. However, I remember how depressed I get when I'm in a state of over-commitment and force myself to go through the exercise of filtering everything through purpose. After you go through this exercise, you have to decide for yourself: Is your purpose off? Or, is the way that you're making decisions off? Only you will know that truth.

Next, think about a major decision in your life. This can be something that has already happened, something that is happening right now, or a decision you foresee making in the future. Think about how, if you employed your purpose statement, you would make that decision. Employing your purpose statement should make the decision-making process easier if your purpose statement is accurately defined. When faced with a decision, does your greater purpose point to a clear pathway? Or does it cause more confusion? If the latter is true, you may have to revisit and revise your purpose statement.

> **"There is NEVER a final draft of a purpose statement."**

THE LAST STEP NEVER ENDS!

The last step in the purpose statement process is to constantly revisit your purpose. This may be hard for people who do not like ambiguity, but you have to remain open to the fact that over time, your purpose will likely evolve. What you write down after your first purpose-centered reflection probably should not be your final draft. In fact, there is never a final draft of a purpose statement. The way to make sure you apply this last step of constant iteration is to go back to step one: reflect often. It took me years to distill down my sense of purpose into the statement I now carry with me everywhere I go.

During law school, my purpose statement was to "use my blessings, opportunities, and experiences to impact the lives of others," and I now say with great confidence that, "My purpose is to shift power to marginalized communities." Throughout time, I realized that the purpose statement of using my blessings, opportunities, and experiences to impact the lives of others was not specific enough. It was more about HOW I lived out my purpose, versus WHAT I hoped to do with my purpose. So, it evolved. I know that my purpose statement is likely to get even more defined in the future, or maybe even change.

The GREATEST thing about a purpose statement is that it is designed to evolve as you learn more about yourself and the world around you.

In this chapter, we learned the importance of reflection, some methods to incorporate reflection into your life, why it's critical to write a purpose statement, how to test your purpose statement, and the need for reiteration. Living a life of purpose and trying to change the world is not easy. Having clarity of purpose is essential if you want to live a lifestyle that is committed to having a positive impact in the world!

ACTIVE REFLECTION:

1. When will you have a proper reflection on purpose? Can you schedule a whole day right now?

2. Which methods of reflection are best suited to your personality? What's holding you back from incorporating at least one reflection technique into your day, every day?

3. How would you write your purpose statement right now?

4. Does your draft purpose statement make it through the following checks: intuitive, loved ones, calendar, and decision check. Where does it get stuck?

5. What do you learn from testing out your draft purpose statement?

6. Go deeper. Is there a big decision that already happened or is approaching that you test your purpose statement on?

7. What will you do to continue to iterate your purpose statement?

PART TWO:
Hustle

To have the courage,
resilience, curiosity, and
initiative tc get it done.

CHAPTER THREE:
Hustle

Let us make our future now and let us
make our dreams tomorrow's reality.

-Malala Yousafzai

"The Purposeful Hustler is COURAGEOUS, curious, resilient, and action-oriented."

DEANNA SINGH

I f living out one's purpose was easy, everyone would be doing it. But it is not easy. Even if you know what your purpose is (hopefully you're close if you read through section one!), you might not know how to live in that purpose. That is where hustle comes in to play. Purpose is WHY you do something. Hustle is HOW you get it done. Knowing your purpose but now knowing how to put it into action sounds like a nightmare. Let's learn how to activate your purpose through hustle!

WHAT IS HUSTLE?

One definition of the word hustle focuses on using backhanded tactics, lying, cheating, hurting others, or being generally self-serving. This side of hustle exists (and these are such negative connotations that I questioned using the word in the book title), but, in my mind, this perspective is limited. I have witnessed another side of hustle—a positive, energizing side. I have seen how people can use hustle to break traditional molds and make a positive social impact. In my experience, hustle is the driving force behind change.

In this book, I don't focus on the type of hustle that's associated with negative connotations. If your hustle is tied to selfish interests, you're not a Purposeful Hustler. Instead, I focus on the type of hustle that athletes, change-makers, and

"Purpose is WHY you do something. Hustle is HOW you get it done."

energized leaders use. This is a propelling force that drives people to keep going, explore all angles of a problem, and not give up. The Purposeful Hustler is an agent for positive change. The Purposeful Hustler is courageous, curious, resilient, and action-oriented.

WHY HUSTLE?

People approach me because they not only want to gain a better understanding of their purpose but also want to know how to activate it. They want to learn practical techniques they can use to stay deeply embedded in purpose. They ask a lot of interesting questions about how to deal with failure, fear, money, relationships, and the calendar. They might not know it, but what they are really asking me about is my hustle. Your hustle is essentially the way you choose to move in the world. It is how you get things done. It is a hustle because it is constantly in motion, evolving and stretching.

WHAT ARE THE BENEFITS OF LEARNING TO HUSTLE?

When people add a little hustle to their game, they are able to accomplish a lot more. Over and over again, I have seen this pattern. Someone approaches me because they are exhausted. They are working or living in a space that does not maximize their full potential. We get through identifying their purpose, and every time they talk about their purpose, their eyes light up. They are excited to talk about what moves them at their core, but they often express that they feel depleted before they even begin. Why? Because while they are happy to identify their purpose, they are overwhelmed by the prospect of figuring out how to live in it.

Sadly, some choose to resign themselves to staying where they are. But others, the ones determined to become Purposeful

Hustlers, start to mix a little hustle into their lives. With hustle, people turn their ship around 180 degrees in very little time. They are able to push past their fears and perceived obstacles and start making change. When I meet with these individuals after they've shifted their lives and incorporated a little hustle into their game, they may still be a bit exhausted, but they are also joyful. When they enter the room, I can feel that something has changed.

What are the basic elements of leveraging your hustle to achieve your purpose? Here are my top three:

Actualize Your Dreams. It is not hard to dream. You can sit around and daydream all day and nothing will change. It is difficult to turn those dreams into reality. Dreaming is important. It is important to be able to see the world for what it could be, not just what it is. But dreaming without action will not yield anything. When you learn the art of the Purposeful Hustle, you learn how to push things out of your head and into reality. The person who wants to start a writing program in her neighborhood doesn't just talk about it. She imagines what the room will look like, knows what she would put on the syllabus, and thinks about the resources she can tap into. She stops dreaming about it and actually starts to teach the class.

Activate. When you are a Purposeful Hustler you will learn how to do things without waiting for permission. When you are trying to make the world a better place, sometimes you have to just do it. Sometimes, people who are waiting

"Your HUSTLE is essentially the way you choose to move in the world."

around for permission don't even know who they are waiting for permission from (oftentimes, they are waiting for themselves!). When you are hustling in your purpose, you not only take action, you build momentum that energizes you and propels you toward your purpose. You get into what a lot of people will call flow—time almost feels like it is on a different continuum because you are highly motivated to see your purpose realized. You aren't moving because you were told to or because you should, but because you feel like you have to! You feel invigorated.

Instead of grumbling about the decay that is happening around the block, the Purposeful Hustler gathers up a few other retired people and starts putting in flower beds around the whole block. They don't wait for someone to speak to them, they go and speak to their neighbors and enlist the help of local kids. Their actions may have a domino effect (people begin to take pride in the gardens, the neighborhood gets cleaner, etc.), but they will never realize these outcomes until they stop thinking and start acting.

Lead. A natural side effect of hustling in your purpose is that you will inspire others to do the same. You will notice right away that people who are watching your Purposeful Hustle will want to know how they can join you. People will start wanting to meet with you and ask you the very questions we are working through in this book. Many will admire the way you are living your life and come to you for guidance about how they, too, can make a change! Just by exemplifying Purposeful Hustle, you will help others step outside their comfort zones. I know a young person who took the initiative to write about her incredible life experience and share it with the world. Even though she was in high school, she started getting calls from all across the community to be a keynote speaker. Though she didn't intend to be a leader, her boldness and clarity of purpose rocketed her to a position of leadership.

Now that you've been introduced to the basic elements of Purposeful Hustle, I want to dive into the origins of my personal hustle and discuss what I learned from my greatest hustler influencers: my parents.

THE ROOTS OF MY HUSTLE

My parents taught me the virtuous side of hustle and helped me build my beginner's toolkit. They showed me how to hustle and provided plenty of opportunities for me to practice. Even though my parents are both driven, motivated people, they have plenty of differences. My mother grew up in the housing projects on Milwaukee's Northside; my father was raised in a small village in India. When they met, they did not share a language or a religion, but they had one very important thing in common: they both knew how to hustle.

Before she was married, my mother was, by her standards, "doing it." She had landed a coveted factory job and was a great worker. When she got the job, it was the first time she had a little bit of money in her pocket. She wanted to live a lifestyle different than the one she had grown up in, but she was judicious with her money. Her Afro was fly, but she learned to do it herself instead of going to a shop. She bought herself a fly car, but it was a used Monte Carlo. She had a fly apartment, but she shared it with her brother. She was always stylish, but she upcycled her second-hand store finds. Her desire to be fly was secondary to her commitment to shed the scarcity she had always known. Instead of marrying young and starting a family like most of her peers, she decided to wait. She wanted to have money, start saving, and avoid having to struggle to make ends meet.

At the time, my father was also trying to blaze his own path. He was supposed to get married and continue to help run the family farm in India, but he had different plans. He secured traveling money by saving and borrowing, and he also managed to secure his grandmother's permission to travel to the U.S. (she was an important voice in the family). Open about his desire to live abroad, my father created a buzz in the village, which fueled his ambitions even further because he wanted to prove to everyone that he would achieve his dreams. With his grandmother's permission, a few hundred dollars, and two outfits, my father managed to get to Canada and, later, Milwaukee, Wisconsin.

Milwaukee was the only place in America where he knew somebody—a distant relative who owned a gas station. He boarded a bus in Seattle with a loaf of bread. At each terminal stop, he would get fountain water. No one tried to talk to him—the strange man in foreign clothes. He couldn't speak English anyway, so the three-day ride passed in silence. All he had was a phone number for his relative and the blind faith that his long journey would not be in vain.

Miraculously, my father found his relative in Milwaukee and began working at his gas station. It was in that gas station where my parents met. My mother often stopped there on her way to or from work, and she began to notice my father's handsome dark eyes and long straight black hair. In turn, my father began to notice my mother's beautiful almond eyes, thick black afro, and sense of style. With an eye for fashion, she often came to the station dressed to the nines. My father must have appreciated American-style clothing because he also began sporting bell bottoms!

Though my father barely spoke English, my parents would converse as best they could at the gas station. Soon, my mother realized that my father was basically living there. She started bringing him homemade food to replace his diet of candy and chips, and soon their pleasantries turned into outings—not dates, more like tutorial sessions. They would go to my mother's apartment and sit in front of the television. My father would ask, "Peggy, what is the meaning of that?" And she would explain what was happening on the screen. These little lessons not only improved my father's English but helped form a bond between the two of them. After knowing each other for just three months, they married, still barely able to communicate in the same language, but certain they were meant to be together (their intuition must have been spot-on, because, after four decades, they're still together). One year after they married, I would come along, and my parents would have to get even more serious about their hustle.

My father made cents for each dollar that came into the gas station. My mother's factory job paid the bills and allowed her to taste a better lifestyle, but she was only paid slightly above minimum wage. Despite these limitations, they had lofty goals. They wanted to save enough money to buy a house and put me in a school district that would pave my way to college.

In those days, there was no end to their creative hustles. My father started to pick up any side job he could find. He drove a taxi until he got robbed. He took discarded stained-glass windows and resold them. My mother took on extra shifts at the factory and also started working at the gas station. She would leave her shift at the factory, go to the gas station, and continue to work there.

Every week, my mother would bring her check home and give it to my father, instead of spending it on the fun frivolities of her 20s. My father would combine her earnings with the bundle of bills and smattering of coins he made throughout the week and then deposit it all into their savings account. There were no new shoes, no restaurants, no unnecessary excursions. Just work. Just savings.

When I was around two years old, a friend of the family bequeathed my mother an old box freezer. My parents put the freezer in their apartment and, forever hustling, decided to start making bags of ice in it. They would buy bundles of clear plastic bags and ties, fill the bags with water, and put them in the freezer. The next morning, they would sell those bags of ice at the gas station. When the landlady discovered their ice selling hustle, she told them she was raising the rent. They couldn't afford the raise, so they moved out. My father wanted my mother to stay with my grandmother, but his pride would not allow him to also stay in his in-law's home. Instead, he stayed at the gas station. But my mother is just as stubborn, and she wanted her family together. So, my mother, father, and I all ended up sleeping on the floor of the gas station until my parents found another apartment they could afford.

Then they started hosting. A lot. Other people—mostly men from my father's village in India—made their way to our small apartment. The men all slept in the living room of our one-bedroom apartment. There was always someone sleeping on the floor or the couch. They had come to America, like my father, to try to build a new life, so my parents offered them jobs. The hustles of my mother and father went beyond themselves and their immediate family. They aimed to help elevate an entire group of people.

With the steady flow of working house guests, my parents

realized they could keep the gas station open 24 hours, and the men could start saving money too. A win-win. Keeping the store open around the clock made it more competitive, and my parents were eventually able to lease and then buy the gas station.

While other gas station operators were paying for people to come and clean the gas station and do improvement work, my parents did it on their own. My father and mother have taught themselves how to do every kind of improvement you can imagine--flooring, ceiling work, plumbing, painting, lawn care. They even stocked the refrigerators themselves and let the delivery drivers pay them on the side.

Their hustle even extended to me. Instead of paying for a babysitter to watch me, I would get ping-ponged to whatever adult was not working. I was always on the move, shifting between the one car we shared (amongst ourselves and our guests) and the bus. When I was still young, I worked behind the gas station counter. I learned how to count money, turn on gas pumps, tell the difference between Marlboro Lights and Regulars, and restock a commercial refrigerator...all before I went to kindergarten.

I stood at the ankles of this gaggle of hardworking immigrants and my mother and watched them work themselves to near exhaustion every day. They were always looking for new ways to improve their hustle, so they could realize their dreams. I was there when they pooled their money to buy another store, when they curled up on the gas station floor to sleep, when they received letters from their families and fought through homesickness, when people called and asked them to do fun things and they passed. I picked up a lot about how to have an honest hustle. From my caretakers in those early years, I learned firsthand what it meant to be courageous, curious, resilient, and action-oriented.

It should be no surprise that I started to flex my hustle moves at a pretty young age, but my initial hustles were far from altruistic. My first one, that I know of, involved creating a consistent flow of Big Macs. I devised a plan at age three to get all the adults to take me to McDonald's, without finding out that I had already been. If I played my cards right, I could get my father to take me on the way to the gas station in the morning and my uncle to take me on the way home at night. My Big Mac scheme lasted until my grandmother discovered my stockpile of happy meal toys.

When I was four, I got a little buggy Flintstone car, the kind you have to peddle. The kids in the apartment complex all came to see my new wheels and ask for a ride! The car was the talk of our little square, and I decided to handle the other kids' requests to play with it by "letting" them drive me around. I would take bids from my friends, collecting candy or coins. Apparently, I needed their fun to be worth my while. The Flintstone car hustle lasted until a crying child reported my scheme to his mother, who then called my mother. That phone call ended my non-altruistic scheme, but I'd had a good run.

During elementary school, my hustle skills became more noble and started to turn toward being purposeful. I decided to get my peers away from the couch (and endless hours of Super Mario!) and immersed in activities. Essentially, I started a mini summer camp. I told the neighborhood kids to come over every day, and I would set up activities for us. The summer camp I organized was prior to Pinterest, and truth be told, the internet altogether, so the activities were not that impressive—the crowd favorite game was one called "Hit Me," in which the children threw balled up socks at me! But my little summer camp became a hit, not only with the children, but with the adults too.

My hustle background taught me that there are a few key attributes every Purposeful Hustler needs:

1. **Courage.** In order to make the changes they made, my mother and father had to walk into a lot of uncomfortable spaces. They were not foolish people, but to an untrained eye, it probably looked like they were acting impulsively. That would be an inaccurate assessment. They took big risks, but they were calculated. It was a big deal for them to get married, live in the gas station, and then keep their store open for 24 hours. They knew they were putting a lot on the line and made sure they could shore up as much as possible in case their plans failed.

2. **Curiosity.** My parents are curious people, eager to learn. When they did not know how to do something, like pulling electrical wiring through a new building, they made an effort to learn. They showed me that you don't have to be an expert in everything before you make a move. And, just because you haven't done something before, doesn't mean you can't try it. You have to be willing to take some risks.

3. **Resiliency.** My parents had some breaks, but luck only made up about 1% of their successes. The other 99% came from persevering, even when times were tough. They had long days—sometimes staying at work for multiple days when they were short on workers—and performed hard manual labor, like putting in tile floors or stocking refrigerators. They also failed. Some products did not sell, new business locations ended up being duds, and people they trusted let them down. But they did not let their failures stop them from

trying and when they failed, they got back up again. They were not afraid of taking on challenges when it meant that those challenges would get them closer to their dreams.

4. **Initiative.** You will never have a flawless plan, enough time, or enough money. There were times when my parents had one of those things, and times when they had none. But they figured out how to move around nimbly, to make their seconds count, and to do things on a dime.

Y ou don't learn
how to master
the HUSTLE from
the sidelines. You
learn how to hustle
by doing.

I had the advantage of watching my parents live out their hustle, but that advantage is not why I have been able to master my hustle. In my experience,

This next section of the book will break down these four characteristics of a Purposeful Hustler so you can apply the lessons to your life. Conveniently, these characteristics will give us the opportunity to address the areas where most people get stuck—the places that keep them from realizing their purpose. I will share the techniques I have seen Purposeful Hustlers master throughout the years to counteract the most common obstacles.

After reading these following chapters, you will understand how to build a Purposeful Hustle that has:

1. Courage: (For the person who is afraid of losing the title, prestige, and/or the comfort of their current standing).

2. Curiosity: (For the person who feels that they don't have the right credentials).

3. Resiliency: (For the person who is afraid of failure).

4. Initiative: (For the person who doesn't have it all figured out).

ACTIVE REFLECTION:

1. Is there a gap between your dreams and reality? What can you do to bridge that gap?

2. What is preventing you from taking action? What is making you feel stuck?

3. Do you consider yourself a courageous person? If yes, where does your courage come from? If not, what is driving your fears?

4. How curious are you? Do you put yourself on quests for knowledge? Do you ever get stuck in the research phase? What makes you curious?

5. Are you resilient? When you fail, how fast can you recover? What mechanisms do you use to recover?

6. Do you take initiative? If yes, where do you get your drive from? If not, what stops you?

CHAPTER FOUR:

Be Courageous

(For the person who is afraid of losing the
title, prestige, and/or the comfort of their
current standing)

Do one thing every day
that scares you.

-Eleanor Roosevelt

Having an effective hustle involves taking risks. You're going to experience adversity, uncomfortable situations, or even confrontation. You might wonder if you're making the right decision for yourself and your future. You may face financial risks. The key is to meet those challenges with courage. Easier said than done, right? Fortunately, courage is something that people can develop over time.

I've taken many actions during my career that might be considered courageous (or, to an outsider, borderline reckless), but they were always calculated. And always guided by my purpose. I remember one incident that got me thinking a lot about calculated courage and how others can apply it to their own Purposeful Hustle...

"You are so courageous," one of my mentors told me.

I was a little taken aback by the compliment. "Thanks," I said. "I guess I never thought about leaving a great job as courageous, maybe foolish, but not courageous."

I paused and let my thoughts linger on what my mentor had said. *Was* I being courageous? Sure, maybe a little...but I had also simply been spurred into action by my purpose.

The day before, I had walked into my supervisor's office and resigned. Resigning had not been easy, but I was confident I was making the right choice. The role, at the beginning, was in direct alignment with my purpose, but it had become clear that the company was headed in a direction that would move it out of

DEANNA SINGH

alignment with my purpose. I had felt terrific about the work I did for the company up until that point and was disappointed that I could no longer continue doing the work I loved. I was also keenly aware of the fact that by leaving this job I was walking away from a majority of my family's income, an incredible team I had recruited, an idea I had created but would not have the joy of bringing to full execution, a steady paycheck, and a prestigious title.

However, even in the midst of all that unpredictability, I was certain the time had come to move on. Why? Because my purpose radar was on red alert. I was getting off the purpose track.

To me, following my purpose was my only option, but my mentor reminded me during our phone call that my actions were far from the norm:

"I said courageous," my mentor continued, "because many people stay in a position that is not aligned with their purpose for their WHOLE life, Deanna."

The thought horrified me. Why would someone continue to work in a role that was in opposition to their purpose?

To make her point, my mentor started listing people in our mutual circles that were in roles that did not support their purposes.

After I hung up the phone, a scary realization hit me: Staying in roles and positions that are not aligned with purpose is the norm. People do this all the time. They get comfortable in a position and let the need to be aligned with their purpose fade into the background. It seemed my mentor was right: I was living the exception. I wondered why.

Then I thought about how scary it could have been to leave my job without all the reservoirs of courage I've built up over the years. It would be scary to make a leap of faith if I was not grounded in a bigger purpose and confident that staying aligned to my purpose is always the best choice. I have had a lot of practice over the years and I want to share with you how I built that reservoir and how you can too.

I can vividly remember times when I felt that the fear of following my purpose would swallow me whole. For the sake of sticking to my purpose, I've often had to go against the grain, and that can give root to a lot of doubt. I can remember being afraid of what people would say, losing my rung on the career ladder, making the wrong choice, failing in a new endeavor, and not having a steady paycheck and health insurance. It didn't help that I also had a terrible experience early in my career.

I had a boss that I looked up to and respected, but when I told him I was going to accept another job offer, he berated me. I tried to explain that this new job would enable me to have a greater impact and was more aligned with my purpose, but he started screaming and cursing. I had never before witnessed that terrifying and aggressive side of him. To this day, whenever I think about moving on, I remember how scary it was to be in that office with him towering over me in anger. But now, when it is time to realign myself with my purpose, I tap into my reservoirs of courage and focus on my larger calling. While transitions are still hard, they are no longer as debilitatingly scary.

STOMP OUT YOUR FEARS

People mistakenly think that those who are "courageous" have no fears. That is far from the truth. Everyone has fears. Purposeful Hustlers are not fearless; they know how to make their fears MEAN less. How do you make your fears mean less? Whenever my fear

"**P**urposeful
Hustlers
are NOT fearless; they
know how to make
their fears **MEAN**
less. "

monster rears its head, I deploy three simple steps. I have found that this technique has the power to shrink my fears and make them seem more manageable, and it gives me a tool to prevent or mitigate adverse outcomes.

1. List out all your fears.
2. Rank them by probability
3. Identify mitigation strategies

Let's look at each of these steps more closely. **First: Write down all your fears**. Write down the big and the small things. This list should be COMPREHENSIVE. Here were some of the things on my list from when I was contemplating resigning:

- My team, the people I cared deeply about, are going to hate me and not understand why I am leaving

- My reputation will be ruined; people will say I got fired.

- I won't be able to say why I moved on without sounding disparaging to the organization (the opposite of what I want to do) or foolish.

- My family and I will have to totally change our lifestyle because of the decrease in income.

- My superiors will throw all my stuff in my office out the window.

- My boss will flip out and start screaming at me.

- I will regret leaving.

- I am overreacting; things are going to line back up to my purpose.

I could go on and on with the list of things I was scared of, but you get the point. The exercise of thinking about worst-case scenarios does not come easily for me. I am an eternal optimist, and I don't like thinking about gloomy things, but when I'm in danger of straying from my purpose, I make myself go there. I try to think about all the things that could go wrong. As difficult as this exercise can be, it forces me to face the potential consequences head-on. It's like a movie scene that shows the littlest person facing down the big, scary person, only to discover that the scary person is really no one to fear. When I list out the consequences, even the ones I find most terrifying, just looking at them makes them smaller.

Next: Rank the probability of each item on your list actually coming true. After I write my doom and gloom list, I go through each point and try to ascertain the likelihood of each fear happening. Going through this step is not complicated probability work. I keep it simple and mark each item as a high, medium, or low.

For example, of all the things I was worried about before quitting my job, my team relationships were the most prominent concern. I started having nightmares about what would happen to them. I felt like I was abandoning them. Another thing that was marked high on my list was the fear that my family's budget would change. This was bound to happen, at least in the short term. Some of our plans and savings goals would have to be put on hold, and we would have to review our spending habits.

On my "medium fears" list was the fear of overreacting. As a drama kid and theater-lover, I have a flair for drama. But, in this case, I was certain that my feelings were not rooted in some irrational place. I had been observing the way things were going and was frustrated by how things were being handled. When I had tried to share my sentiments and concerns, I was not heard. I was being asked to co-sign on things that didn't align with my beliefs, and I felt like my integrity was being tested. So, while the thought that I was being overly dramatic was not one I could rule out right away, I didn't think the probability was terribly high.

In the low category was fear that someone would throw all my things out the window! I had witnessed some erratic behavior at the organization but opening my office window was almost always a two-person job and I could not imagine two people conspiring to throw my stuff out. I also didn't have anything terribly toss-worthy, and I had a solid relationship with my colleagues. The probability of multiple people participating in throwing my things out seemed low to non-existent but the concern was still on my list.

Third: Identify mitigating strategies for each fear. Reckoning with the real possibility of your fears coming true can definitely be anxiety-producing. As soon as you start down a path of doom, it's easy to follow the path all the way down. That's why the second step has to be coupled with the third step IMMEDIATELY! After you have discerned the probability of something happening, begin listing strategies to mitigate each of the fears. Mitigation is a word typically used in legal settings, but it is appropriate for this exercise. When you mitigate something, you do things to make any potential consequences less severe.

When coming up with mitigation strategies before leaving my non-aligned job, I began with my biggest fear: losing or damaging the relationships with people I had hired to be on my team. I went through each of the people I was concerned about, and I thought through what I could do to independently support them. I also realized that one of the reasons I cared so deeply about them was because they were the kind of people who were wildly intelligent and sensitive to their purposes. If anyone would understand why I needed to move on, they would. Making the choice to leave was also a chance to demonstrate the kind of leader I aspire to be—the kind that stays true to my purpose, values integrity over a paycheck, and works from a place of joy, not fear!

Then, I tackled my second big fear: a major and swift change to my family's budget. I wrote up a new budget and shared it with my husband to get his input about the adjustments we had to make in the immediate and long-term. Creating a new budget was a helpful exercise. The budget allowed us to affirm that we still had the same goals but needed to temporarily shift priorities. We also realized that many of the things we had to change would have no impact on our day-to-day living. We would have to scale back from some of our bigger goals and be more discerning with purchases, but the budget was doable.

To mitigate the "medium fear" that I was overly-dramatic, I created a list of troubling things I had witnessed and shared them with my inner circle. I wanted to gauge how they, all more level-headed than I, would respond. As it turns out, they were even more incensed than I was. One of my closest friends said without any prompting, "What is happening is totally against the purpose of your life." Writing the list helped me see patterns that I had been missing as I was living through it all.

Lastly, before I issued my resignation, I filled up a box of my possessions from my office that were precious and irreplaceable and put that box in the trunk of my car. I figured if all hell broke loose, which was a LOW probability, I would at least have the things that held a lot of value.

Doing all these things—thinking about how I could continue to support the team, redoing our personal budget, talking to friends, and taking my valuables out of the office—were critical components of my mitigation process.

Going through this mitigation process made me feel more in control. It also helped me identify the potential consequences of resigning and enabled me to trust my ability to get through them. Because I was not acting rashly, my resignation came from a place of confidence and clarity. It would have been much harder to be courageous without having a mitigation strategy in place.

After you have an idea of what you can do to mitigate the things that make you nervous, there are some ways to tackle that mitigation list. One way is to reorder it, listing the smallest tasks first. Unless tasks need to be done in a certain order, do the things that will take you five minutes or less, then tackle the ten-minute tasks, and so on. I have found that approaching your tasks in this way helps create momentum.

Another strategy is to take care of the scariest item on your mitigation list first. If you go ahead and do the hardest thing first, the rest will, by design, be easier. Doing it this way might even render the remaining little things unnecessary. You may realize after the big thing is done that the rest of your fear list was just a hoax—your mind playing tricks on you.

Activating your mitigation list will allow you to take action, instead of remaining stuck in your stress. I could have waited to share my decision with my team and my superior, but once I knew I was going to leave, I took the very first opportunity to share the news. I knew that the longer I held on to my decision, the more doubt and fear would play in my mind. I also realized that once I made my decision public knowledge, I would begin to find out the actual consequences of my action, instead of imagining worst-case scenarios.

Though I attempted to have some measure of control during my exit, I still had to deal with a lot of unknowns. For many of us, not knowing what lies ahead is downright terrifying, but being true to your purpose isn't always easy. Purposeful Hustlers know fear. They wrestle with fear. Fear keeps them up at night. But they do not let fear stand in the way of doing what they ultimately know that they must do to stay in their purpose.

COURAGE TRAINING

We have talked here about what happens when you have the time to build your courage before you have to use it. But there will be other times when you are not given that space and time, and you have to act in the moment.

The only way to be successful during those unanticipated challenges is to constantly practice living in your purpose. This is just like training for a sport. During the off-season, athletes continue to train. Why? Because they know that even if they have meticulous plans for their upcoming games, there are going to be situations that will require them to perform in the moment. Similarly, if you choose to act from a place of purpose every single day, your purpose muscle will be well-developed and ready when you are put on the spot. You'll still have to call upon your reservoir of courage, but hopefully doing so will feel *natural.*

I get tested on the spot regularly. The most common instance for me is when I am with people of great power who *believe* they are helping others but often neglect to listen to the voices of those whom they intend to serve. In these cases, I know that if I don't speak out, those in power will continue to push their viewpoints onto those who are not at the table (the underserved populations that they *intend* to help). Since I am committed to shifting power to marginalized communities, my purpose will not let me stay quiet. I have to be prepared to speak out, even when it is uncomfortable.

When I am at a loss for what to do or say, my most common exercise is to state that out loud. I will say "I assume everyone has good intentions, but I am really uncomfortable right now. My purpose in life is to help shift power to marginalized communities and right now this [fill in the blank—the way the conversation is going, the way we are acting, etc.] seems misaligned. I am not sure what to do, can you all help me?"

What this does is put everyone on notice that I am uncomfortable and allows for everyone to reflect and get into problem-solving mode with me. While this makes me vulnerable in that moment, it also gives me peace, because there is nothing worse than feeling that when your purpose was tested, you did nothing.

ACTIVE REFLECTION:

1. What's holding you back from making a certain decision?

   a. List out all the reasons you are scared.

   b. What is the probability (low, medium, high) that the things on your list will come true?

   c. What could you do to mitigate those fears?

2. When you feel put on the spot, what can you lean back on (the motivating factors in your life)? Where have you already demonstrated courage? How can you tap into that courage reservoir going forward?

FEAR MITIGATION

I am afraid of		
Fear	Probability (High, Medium, Low)	Mitigation Strategies

Chapter Five:

Be Curious

(For the person who feels that they
don't have the right credentials)

I am learning all the time. The
tombstone will be my diploma.

-Eartha Kitt

Sometimes the quest for knowledge can become an inhibitor. We can become beholden to a false truth: that we must acquire as much knowledge as possible before acting. In reality, no one can ever know *everything* about a given subject, but I have found that many people delay acting in their purpose and moving forward because they feel like they don't have enough expertise. The Purposeful Hustler values knowledge, but they are comfortable gaining it as they go. They recognize that accumulating knowledge on their journey can help them build their hustle and give them the skills they need to effectively make an impact.

More than once, I've plunged into projects where I've had to learn on the fly, but I've always managed to find the necessary resources to keep my head above water and make a difference. The journey isn't always comfortable, and I've often doubted my abilities, but the payoffs can be huge. I clearly remember one pivotal moment that compelled me to strike out in an entirely new direction, despite my lack of knowledge. It all started around a boardroom table, while working in the field of philanthropy...

I loved the work I did as a philanthropist. I loved being able to give people the resources they needed to help realize their mission and try new, innovative methods for magnifying their impact. I loved helping strategize for a better future with fellow change agents. What I didn't love was the feeling that sometimes, despite my best intentions, I was perpetuating the power dynamic that got us into the situations we were trying to overcome.

Despite my areas of discomfort, I didn't feel like I was out of my purpose. As an insider I was able to help organizations from a place of empathy, and address issues that others may not have even considered. But that does not mean I did not question the work. During one particular meeting with other child advocates, the imbalance of power dynamics became especially painful. We were talking about children of color, boys in particular, and what we could do collectively to change some of the most pressing disparities. I was deeply disturbed by the way people were talking about children in that meeting. They were not talking about them as beautiful, intelligent, curious little people. They were being referred to as statistics, as problems. I got up during that meeting and tried to change the course of the conversation. I made an impassioned plea to the room to remember that we had a responsibility to represent the children with dignity. Another woman across the room echoed my sentiment. I thought we were making progress, but the next person who talked took us right back to the same negative, deficit-based language, and the conversation continued with people dehumanizing children through the use of negative statistics. I kept thinking, what if my children, or any children for that matter, were in this room. What would they think about how people were talking about them?

Around this time in my life, one of the other things actively occupying my psyche was that my children, my two little brown boys, were on the cusp of leaving the sanctity of their home, about to start school. The mounting realization that I did not have the ability to protect them was gnawing at my soul. It was demoralizing and was weighing on me in an almost indescribable way. I was overwhelmed. I felt a rage boil inside of me.

The rage did not start at that meeting; it had been mounting for some time. This idea, that we have to change our mindset about the ways we talk about children, particularly our children of color, was not new. In college, the title of my senior thesis was, "Raise Men, Not Prisoners," in which I argued that, as a society, we are complicit in creating a prophecy with our words and depictions that some young men of color are tragically fulfilling, and people in power are reinforcing through policy and actions. My rage was also being fueled by the fact that there are so many violent crimes happening at the hands of people, particularly police, that are rooted in the widely held belief that men of color are to be assumed guilty and dangerous—they are dehumanized to the point of caricature.

And here we were in a meeting, where we were supposed to be talking about how to change those dynamics, and the people in the room were further perpetuating them. I could feel my insides start to swell, and I had vivid images of turning over desks and throwing chairs. I could see the headline: "Foundation Executive Turns Incredible Hulk"...but the instant before I boiled over, I picked up a pen. I started to write a letter to my boys. The letter basically said: *If something were to happen to your father and me, it is really important for you to realize how amazing you are. You need to know that the things we say about you—things like you are creative, smart, and beautiful—are true. You need to know that the world out there is not going to reflect those images to you, so you have to know them yourself. You have to know that this is true.*

I continued writing after the meeting ended and people left. I stayed until I was finished and took the note home. I turned it into a PDF and overlaid the words on top of pictures of my children.

My blood started flowing more naturally in my body, and I thought I would give my sons this letter and be able to return to work like normal.

But the opposite happened. The feelings of frustration kept growing. My brain began to desperately look for ways to insert myself more fully into the solution. I thought about my sons, nephews, husband, father, grandparents, and all the other little children I have had the honor of working with over the years. The pain in my heart was so strong, on some days it felt debilitating. I felt helpless in the face of such a big problem. I even wondered what the point of trying was. But my brain wouldn't rest; my heart wouldn't let it.

One day, in its quest for an answer, I came across disturbing facts. The University of Wisconsin-Madison's Cooperative Children's Book Center studies the representation of children of color in children's books. In 2015 they found that 73% of books released that year featured white children, while only 14% of the total number of books featured children of color. More books featured inanimate objects than actual children of color. However, our school-aged student population in this country is **MAJORITY** children of color. Something was off. Shouldn't children of color be able to find books that feature them too? This was also confusing because any reading teacher will tell you that the number one way to get a child engaged in reading is to help them find themselves in a book—something that they can relate to.

What are we saying to children when they are not represented in our literature? Isn't reading supposed to open their worlds, instead of acting like a gate to block them out? Shouldn't reading give them the freedom to experience anything—a great equalizer? This made me wonder if the letter I wrote to my children was actually a letter to all children. Could I take that letter and make it into a children's book? As I thought about it, I wondered if creating such a book would help me heal the pain in my heart and be part of a meaningful solution.

There was just one problem: I had no idea how to go about creating a book. I didn't think I had the skills, knowledge, or experience.

I was very aware of what I did *not* know. It is safe to say that I had no understanding of ANY of the major required components of the book business. I knew nothing about writing, designing, publishing, marketing, pricing, or selling a children's book. I did not have the credibility that I would need to be taken seriously. I doubted I had the skills needed to get published; I didn't feel like I had the chops to get something into print.

In short, I was temporarily paralyzed by my *perceived* lack of actionable knowledge.

There were so many reasons to NOT do it, and just one reason TO do it: writing the book was directly connected to my purpose. I felt that if I could be a part of changing the narrative around children of color, I could help switch the power dynamics in their favor.

Part of my desire to take action also stemmed from my personal awareness of the power of the written word. When I was young, I would hide in the closet and turn the light on so I could read past bedtime. I loved how reading transported me, but it wasn't until high school that I understood how it could make me feel powerful. For the first time, I read a book that featured a girl of color. I read and re-read that book because of how much I identified with the little girl in it. It was a transformative experience. Reflecting on that time, I realized I wanted as many children as possible to also feel the same sense of power I had gained through reading.

I decided to stop thinking about what I didn't have and start focusing on what I did. I began taking an asset-based, not deficit-based, approach to the idea and soon realized I did have some knowledge and skills that could prove useful. For the other areas, I could call upon knowledgeable individuals for assistance.

Using my publishing journey as an example, let's examine four different steps you can take when confronted with a situation in which you lack knowledge or resources.

1. START WITH WHAT YOU KNOW

Teachers are often taught Bloom's Taxonomy. One of the central concepts of the taxonomy is that to teach higher-level thinking, you have to start with what a person already knows and then build on that knowledge. The Bloom's Taxonomy framework is considered a best practice within the teaching field and can easily be applied at the individual level too. When thinking about the knowledge you need, start with what you already know.

At first, I was worried that I knew nothing about the publishing process, but then I reframed my mindset and considered what I did know. Here's what I came up with:

- I knew that, as a mother and an educator, finding books with representation is important.

- I knew, based on my own experience, that it was challenging to find children's books that featured positive images of children of color.

- I knew I was not alone. When looking for books, I found a bunch of other parents and educators online who were equally frustrated by the lack of representation. These anecdotal pieces of knowledge were backed up by the research I found on the topic too, like the image depicted earlier in this chapter.

- I knew that few publishing venues focus on creating books with appropriate representation of children of color.

- I knew what kinds of books I liked to read to my children. I knew what they looked like, what they felt like, and how they were structured.

- I knew I could write.

When thinking about your skills do not overlook the obvious things. Start with the basics. For example, can you read and write? Having that skill puts you in a position to access a multitude of different people who might want to engage with you in your quest for social justice. If you can read, you will be able to find people and resources that are naturally aligned with your work. You can search online or look on social media for people who are experts in the field and read what they have to say and/or connect with them. If you can write, that means you can document the experiences you are having and the feedback you receive from others.

I had a student that was charged with organizing a parent group. She was not a parent, and so it made her feel a little odd to have the responsibility, and she didn't know what she could offer the group. However, she quickly realized that the parents did not need or want someone in her role to be a parent—that was at the bottom of the requisite skills for the role. What they wanted was someone to document their needs and concerns, and then be their advocate in the face of the powers that be. They needed her to help them find the research to support what they knew to be true from experience. They also needed her to capture their stories in a concise and compelling way so that leaders would understand their messages and be able to respond. Her largest contribution to that group quickly became her communication skills, and she learned just how valuable they were as a social justice leader.

2. Recognize Your Knowledge and Skills Gaps and Close Them!

After I had clarity on what assets I did have, it was time to look at what I was missing. There were a lot of things I didn't know, mostly relating to the publishing process. I had no idea what publishing entailed, so I decided to start learning. I would spend hours on Google, searching for answers to the questions I had. What is the difference between a traditional press and self-publishing? What is the importance of an ISBN? How do people get their books into major retailers? What makes a children's book successful? This is how I spent my wee hours of the morning. Most of this research and learning was done between the hours of 12 and 2 a.m.

In addition to reading, I started reaching out to others. I connected with published authors I knew. I discovered writers who were working on cool projects and connected to them on social media so I could follow their work. I reached out to a local indie publisher to learn more about their process. I also went to a class hosted by a writer. The class wasn't aimed at writing a children's book, but I was interested in listening to a professional writer discuss her process. I also joined a national organization called the Society for Children's Book Writers and started reading their newsletters. This put me in contact with other great practitioners in the field. There was still a lot I didn't know, but within a few months, I had accumulated enough knowledge to be dangerous and able to make some big decisions that would move the project forward.

What about skills? How do you develop skills you do not have? Publishing a book requires a lot of skills, including editing, interior design, marketing, pricing, and distributing the book. I didn't have many of those skills but felt I could acquire them. For example, I had never made an e-commerce website, but I figured it out by looking at some YouTube videos, using a template from my hosting company, and visiting other sites that I liked. This preliminary knowledge got me to a place where I was able to create my website's framework and bring in a professional to tie the loose ends. I went from a bid of a few thousand dollars to just around $100 to get the initial website up and running.

3. Dare to Ask For Help

One of the most important things to remember when looking at your skill deficits is that there will be a time when the skill does not and probably should not come from you. In those instances, it is imperative to seek out people who do have the necessary skills.

One crucial skill I was missing was the ability to illustrate. I can barely make recognizable stick figures, so illustrating my book was never an option. I had a sense of what I wanted the images to look like, but my vocabulary to explain my ideas was seriously inadequate. I asked some different artists for samples and got a lot of cartoon/superhero figures back—the exact opposite of what I wanted. I wanted the children in my book to look like real children of color, with accurately captured eyes and hair. One time, after spending a lot of time explaining the importance of the children's eyes and hair to an artist, I was given a picture of a bald child with closed eyes. I am not sure if that was a communication issue or if the artist was being cheeky.

After much fruitless searching, I finally stumbled across an image I loved. I spotted it while flipping through social media and was immediately drawn to it. It was perfect—exactly what I had been looking for. I reached out to the artist to see if he would be interested in illustrating my book. No response. My publisher reached out; he said thank you, but he was too busy to take the project. I reached out again. His answer was a polite, "No, thank you." He was too busy with other projects. I continued to follow him on social media and fell even more in love with his work. One day, he posted that he was going to be in a gallery doing portraits.

My whole family and I went to the gallery. My hustle was in full throttle—I would not back down without trying everything! On the way in I asked the kids to turn UP their cuteness to its maximum level. The artist, Ammar, knew who I was immediately. We waited on the side patiently, and when he had a break, with my children beside me, I asked again. This last time, he said yes! The project became as much his as mine once he realized the full scope of what we were doing. His beautiful images grace the pages of *I am a Boy of Color*, and I could not be prouder to have worked with such a talented person.

4. STRENGTHEN YOUR KNOWLEDGE:

There are many ways to strengthen your knowledge and skillset. I have found the following methods to be effective, but everyone learns in different ways. Find the methods that best suit your learning style.

Seek Out Learning Experiences

A lot of people mistakenly think that knowledge can only come through a formal process, and they need to earn some kind of certificate before they can engage in their purpose. One of the most common things I hear from others is that they can't move forward with their purpose until they have obtained their degree. Only a handful of the world's population has access to higher education. As of 2016, only about 7% of people worldwide have a college degree. Having a degree is a privilege (and is, of course, a worthy goal), but it is not a requisite for being a Purposeful Hustler. No degree is needed to follow your purpose;

> Purposeful Hustle is a MINDSET that is free and available to anyone who is seeking it.

It is frustrating when people, young and old, believe they cannot follow their purpose because they have not received a piece of paper telling them they can pursue those dreams. "I do not have my degree yet" is not a viable excuse. Think about this in the inverse—I know a lot of people who have degrees and are not living in their purpose. One does not necessitate the other.

If you have the great honor and privilege of pursuing a degree, awesome! Get it done. But realize that having the degree does not automatically deliver value—it is what you do with the knowledge you have gained that will make a difference. I can speak from experience. I have a lot of degrees, and the knowledge I gained is useful, but we live in the information age Gaining knowledge is not hard. If you want to learn something, there is probably a cheap or free way to do it. Check out a book from the library, watch videos on YouTube, or join an online forum around your topic of interest. Even if you are getting a degree, remember that you can direct your learning by choosing classes that match your purpose or help you gain additional knowledge. In the last six months, through online educational programs, I have learned about aspects of writing, coaching, and digital marketing. I spent less than $30 to gain a wealth of great primary knowledge.

All you need to get started is some basic knowledge and a growth mindset to effectuate change.

DEVELOP A READING LIST

It gives me the shivers to think about how much knowledge is contained in the written word. Just the possibility of gaining knowledge makes libraries one of my favorite places. But the fact that there is so much to read can also be overwhelming. To make my research into the publishing process more manageable, I set aside two hours to put together an ideal reading list. After a few simple Google searches, the list was compiled, and then I spent another hour prioritizing the items.

When you make your own list, don't feel like you have to limit it to just traditional texts; feel free to include other multimedia forms that interest you. After finishing your list, give yourself a restricted amount of time to consume the information. So. if you have two books, ten articles, and five videos, you might allocate how much time you need to get through all of those and then set a limit. I am a fast reader, so I would assume that the two books would take me about 4 hours each (480 minutes), The articles would take about 30 minutes each (total of 300 minutes), and the videos would take about 90 minutes. That is a total of 870 minutes or 14.5 hours. If I only had five hours a week to dedicate to this work, I would give myself three weeks to complete the reading list. If I had a weekend coming up where I could hide away and do two full eight-hour sessions, I would give myself one weekend. Determining how much time it will take you to get through the materials will help you set realistic deadlines and stay on track.

CREATE A SCHEDULE

Here is what WILL happen, without fail. During your research (especially if you are using the internet), you'll come across other things you'll want to explore. Resist changing your initial timetable! Instead, I offer you two suggestions:

1. Think about the research you have already listed and switch out your new discovery with something you already scheduled.

2. Compose your next list.

Do NOT extend your initial time unless you absolutely must. Why am I so adamant about this? Because if you do that now, you will increase the risk of falling into a research rabbit hole, and it will be hard to dig yourself out. There will be times when you will learn something mind-blowing but do your best to refocus your attention on your initial list. I recommend creating a list of things you'd like to explore after your initial research is finished. Only add more time if you find items that are fundamental to what you need to know.

There is an important thing to note here: You do not have to know everything. In fact, you should not know everything. Know enough to be informed and thoughtful, but full knowledge is a wasted effort. Why? Because (1) in this information age it is impossible to dissect everything, and (2) part of your innovative spirit will need to be protected from the constant naysayers. You're bound to find tons of reasons why things didn't work for certain people, and therefore can never work. Don't let your ideas get trampled by those who lack vision and persistence.

Start a Listening Tour

Have you heard of a listening tour? A listening tour is a fancy term to describe going around and talking to people with the goal of learning more about a particular subject. When I want to learn something quickly, I organize a listening tour with various experts. This is a great way to boost your knowledge—talking to practitioners who are already knowledgeable about a particular area of interest. Who comes to mind when you think about the work you'd like to pursue?

It is heartening to see a fresh, curious mind talking to a veteran. I like to hear them swap questions and test each other's premises. People in the social sector do not get the respect they deserve. Most are experts in their fields, even though their expertise has likely been molded by experience, rather than formal training. Their perspective is not only illuminating but necessary for the social change agent who wants to have a real impact. Meet these individuals and learn from them because their credibility has been tested not in ivory towers but through real-life experience. The best way to request a meeting with an expert is simply to ask. I have asked some really important people, totally outside my network, if

I could meet with them and I have rarely been told no. I pose the question like this:

Dear Amazing Practitioner in a Field Related to my Purpose,

I hope you are doing well. I am deeply interested in becoming more engaged in XYZ work, and your name keeps coming up as a leading authority in the area. I was wondering if I could have 15-30 minutes of your time to ask you some questions about a few things I am pondering with the XYZ phase. I am looking for a way to be more involved in an impactful way and would consider your insights valuable. Do you have any time the week of (pick a date 3-4 weeks out, given who you are addressing)?

I would be happy to discuss payment for your time.

Sincerely,
Purposeful Hustler

As part of your listening tour, don't forget to talk to those who are most deeply engaged in work that is similar to your purpose. If you are interested in education, talk to teachers and students. If you are interested in criminal justice, talk to law enforcement officers and people who have been arrested. In other words, don't forget to include the target population you hope to serve alongside on your tour.

To me, including those whom you want to serve on your listening tour is obvious, but I am deeply troubled by how many people skip it. I am often struck by this kind of negligence in my youth engagement work. A lot of people make decisions about young people, but never spend any time with them. I was at an event recently to raise money for a youth organization. Before the event, the table sponsors had a chance to meet with the students. I was excited to see the students and catch up on what was going on in their lives. I didn't know all of them, but I did know some because I had made an effort to meet them before the event. I was shocked when I looked around the room and realized that all the other donors were silently watching me talk to the children, instead of also making an effort to engage with them. Afterward, most of the other key donors admitted that they had never met any of the students or even been to the site. I wondered why they had committed large sums of money to the organization and never made a point to talk to the children. It was great they were supporting the organization, but I wondered how much more effective they could have been if they actually got to know the beneficiaries of their donations!

HAVE AN IMMERSION EXPERIENCE

One of the best ways to learn about something is to totally immerse yourself in the situation. My cousin spent a year in a remote village in India with no electricity. He wanted to see firsthand how the educational system was being deployed in rural and impoverished communities. It wasn't until after he had this experience that he joined the Teach For India team. I had another friend who was interested in the local food movement and how to increase access to healthy foods in low-income neighborhoods. She decided that before she did any work at the policy level, she would spend time working on a farm, developing an understanding of how local food is produced, harvested, and sold. She learned all she could so that she could incorporate that knowledge into her work. Both these young people chose to immerse themselves into the challenges they were hoping to solve and as a result were able to come out of those experiences with more realistic ways to live in their purpose.

VOLUNTEER:

Total immersion is not the only way to gain profound knowledge in your purpose area. You can also learn through volunteering. In fact, I think it is irresponsible to want to engage in social justice work without first seeing how things happen at the ground level. This means you have to spend time with and amongst the people who are directly impacted by the social justice issue you hope to work on. When you volunteer, don't be afraid to step outside your comfort zone. Try to get as close to the action as possible. For example, if you want to get engaged in school reform, volunteer to be an after-school tutor for six months—don't volunteer to help with the annual gala where you will never meet any children.

The Purposeful Hustler is excited to learn. They want to build their knowledge and skillset. They look at their lack of expertise not as an excuse to stay stuck but rather as an opportunity to go deeper and stretch themselves.

Active Reflection:

1. What skills are needed to make the impact you want to make?

2. Which skills do you already have?

3. Which skills can you learn?

4. Which areas will require additional expertise or support?

5. Make a learning plan that you can use to help you get closer to your purpose!

CHAPTER SIX:

Be Resilient

(For the person who is afraid
of failure)

And the day came when the risk to
remain tight in a bud was more painful
than the risk it took to blossom.

-Anaís Nin

A s a Purposeful Hustler, you will fail. That is a fact. If you want to make a big, lasting impact, you will have to take risks, and occasionally those risks will not pay off. Your resiliency will be tested. It is easy to only think about the highs, but it is also important to think about how you are going to handle the lows and shore yourself up for the blows.

I joined the Street Law Program in my second year at Georgetown Law. This turned out to be a foundational experience. It was one of the most challenging things I did during my law school career. Through the Street Law Program, law students go to public schools and teach a yearlong course in law. At Georgetown, some of the students went to teach in the community, but most were assigned to a high school for the year.

I loved participating in the program because it allowed me to immediately pass on what I was learning to other people who did not readily have access to the information. I could teach my students what their rights were, or how to negotiate a lease. I wanted them to be empowered when they thought about the law. This experience left such an impression on me that, before I started my job at Legal Action in Milwaukee, I asked my supervisors if I could have permission to start a local branch of the Street Law Program. I promised I would work on this program during my own time, with my own resources. All I needed in return was their promise to not deter me and let me shift my schedule when I had to be in schools.

Starting the program was grueling. I worked long days to

DEANNA SINGH

"I used my PURPOSE to fuel my hustle."

make it happen. Most of the work on the program was done after a full day of work and a bar exam review. There were three groups I needed to get on board to make the project happen: the school district, the law school, and the local legal community. Each of them provided different challenges.

I started engaging the school districts first because without students there would be no program. One particularly tough day, after having multiple doors shut in my face, I was lovingly told, "Do not take it personally." This was well-intentioned advice, but it was wrong. It was personal. I had come back to Milwaukee not to make an incremental change but to be a part of big change. Milwaukee raised me. I owed the city something! I had spent seven years being actively engaged in the lives of young people and was lost without that connection. It was personal—very personal.

And that is okay. **It is okay to blur the line between the personal and professional.** I have lived my entire career in that space. I don't take off my social justice hat when I get home. I don't take it off when I walk into a corporate building. I blur those lines because if we are honest, they are already blurred. Being intentional about blurring them allows me to show up in a room and be fully myself. When I work, it is always personal, which means that when things happen, they have an effect on me. Challenges test my resolve and my character. They test my resiliency.

While working to start a branch of the Street Law Program, I hit all kind of roadblocks for three months. I tackled each of them aggressively (though professionally as possible) because I had a personal stake in the project—I used my purpose to fuel my hustle. I called all kinds of different people within the school district, in different departments. Some people never returned my phone calls; others told me to try other departments—some that I would later learn were defunct, others that simply were not interested. During my inquiries, I learned that hundreds of Street Law textbooks had been purchased at one point, but no one knew where they had ended up. However, the fact that the district bought them gave me hope that someone, somewhere was interested in the material. So, I persisted.

Finally, I was given a piece of important advice by one knowledgeable individual I had reached out to: "Stop trying to go through the district; go to the schools directly." The contact went even further and gave me the names of teachers I should talk to. He helped me navigate to the people who were the boots-on-the-ground decision-makers. That makes sense to me now, but at the time I thought the most effective way to get things done was to go the top of the organization. The teachers ended up being much more receptive because they were directly connected to the students and realized right away the potential positive impact. Plus, they knew exactly how to play within the larger system. Their influence turned the key.

The second group I had to connect with was the law school. Here again, I found some challenges. I was told that no law students would want to spend their time teaching other children, but I knew that wasn't true. At Georgetown, the Street Law clinic was wildly popular and it was a competitive process to get in. At the time the program had been going for over 30 years.

I decided I needed to connect with students to prove that they indeed wanted to be part of the Street Law Program. I started reaching out to a couple of student organizations and student leaders on campus, including the people who were running the Black Law Student Association and those who had been recognized by the University for doing public interest type work. I also got a hold of the student paper and began looking for people of interest there. When I went to socially-minded events that summer, I made sure to talk to the students I met. I also sought out recent graduates and asked if they thought the program would be a good fit. Eventually, I was able to pull together not just a group of students but a phenomenal group of leaders on campus to be part of the first cohort.

The second challenge at the law school involved making a case for the program to the administration. I can see why they were concerned that I—a recent graduate with no formal legal experience outside my internships—thought I could run a clinical program. I am sure they were also wondering how someone without any teaching credentials to speak of, besides my own experiences, could teach students how to teach others. Those misgivings, coupled with the fact that I already had a full-time job, made it challenging to find a real advocate on campus at first.

The departments I reached out to had no interest in being involved in a clinic or something outside the law school, and the individual professors were already deep in the throes of their own classes or projects. After hitting multiple dead ends at a number of different offices, I finally scored a meeting with the Academic Dean. When I walked into his office I was terrified. He is a highly respected member of the bar, and I was intimidated. I heard he demanded excellence and asked tough questions. But I soon learned that he is deeply passionate about justice. Despite the fact that so many other people had closed the door in my face, he listened to me. He told me that someone else, a former member of the faculty, had tried to start the program years earlier with no success. He shared that he was sad to see it not work out. And then he gave me a great gift. He proposed that we pilot the program for the first year. We decided not to call it a class, but instead made the program an independent study. He handled the administrative side of things and as soon as I was given the green light, we were off. I am deeply grateful to the Dean for staying in my corner as an advocate, and later, as a friend.

The last group I needed on board was my colleagues in the bar association. I wanted them to be excited about the work because I hoped they would be guest speakers, judges for mock trial competitions, and outside advocates for the program. I remember being excited about reaching out to one attorney in particular—a person I had admired from afar. She was, by everyone's measure, a sure win. I spent hours poring over my introduction email, hoping it would wow her. Her response was brutal. When I read the condescending single-spaced, three-page note, I was shocked. I expected her to be the perfect advocate, but she made it clear that she thought the program was dumb and would never work. I sat with her letter a long time, sick to my stomach. She had not even taken the time to punctuate, and many of her assertions were just plain untrue. I was afraid she was going to sabotage me. I printed that stupid letter and read it again and again. I cried. Then I put it aside and went to sleep.

The next morning, I picked the letter back up and sat down with a legal pad. I went through each paragraph, pulled out all of the reasons she said the program was not going to work, and made a list. Then I went through each point and made sure I had a plan to address every one of her concerns. I never talked to her again. I don't even think I replied. That experience was a lesson on many levels. First, it taught me how to use my critics as a tool for making my work stronger. Not all of her points were valid, but they made me realize I needed to improve my pitch. When I reached out to new people about the Street Law Program, I started using language in my introduction to directly address the doubts she raised. This added insight allowed me to move people to an ally position more quickly because I was able to address their doubts head-on.

She also taught me how not to interact with junior people. If she had shared her same concerns in a constructive and encouraging way, I could have skipped the tears and she would have gained an even greater admirer. Being a Purposeful Hustler will naturally make you a leader. It is important that when you are in that space, you do not hurt those around you, especially those that are on your side.

Aside from that woman, most of my colleagues in the bar association were eager to help. Unfortunately, my network was not deep. I remember getting up from a meeting with one lawyer who had agreed to help. As I was packing up my things, he said, "You forgot to ask me the most important question, Deanna." I looked at him, confused. "You should always end a meeting by asking 'Who else should I be talking to?'" I sat back down, and he gave me a list. That afternoon, I sent him a draft email he could use to introduce me to his colleagues. He then sent it out to people he thought would be interested. With only a few minutes of work, my network multiplied overnight.

With the support of the students, administration, and my colleagues from the bar, the Milwaukee Street Law Program became a reality. When the work is personal, it is harder to fail. It is harder to not get back up and try again. Yes, purposeful work will test your resiliency, but it is worth it.

Today, almost a decade has passed since its founding, and the Street Law Program continues to go strong. It is operated by former students who found it too meaningful to let go as they went into private practice. Though I passed the Street Law torch to another director years ago, the program still holds deep meaning for me, and it freaks me out that I almost gave up on it. If I had given up, many young people would not have had the opportunity to flourish in the program.

I have found that setbacks are a reality, but true failure only comes if you give up. The Purposeful Hustler doesn't throw in the towel but keeps at their goals until they are achieved (or at least headed in the right direction). **That is not to say you will not experience small failures, just don't let them get you stuck**.

Confronting Failure

How do you experience many small failures, but end up triumphant in the end? How can you pick yourself up and keep moving forward? Where does this relentless behavior come from? Here is what the Purposeful Hustler does when confronting failure.

First, Purposeful Hustlers embrace failure. We take our temporary failures and squeeze them. When you are doing work that comes from your heart, failure hurts. You feel like you failed not just yourself but the very thing you feel most responsible for in the world. The Purposeful Hustler does not let that pain stop them from moving forward, but they do spend some time, as the kids like to say "in their feelings." I have found that it's healthy to reflect on the emotions of failure and use those deep cuts to propel me forward in my mission. In many ways, the entire existence of the Milwaukee Street Law Program is rooted in a series of failures I experienced while working as a teacher in the Street Law Program in D.C.

When I was teaching in D.C. the high school students didn't choose to be in my law class. It was required. They struggled with some of the concepts and were resistant to the activities I planned. To this day, I think high schoolers are the toughest audience, with middle schoolers being a close second. I had one student who was extra difficult. She kept her head on her desk and wouldn't look at me when I asked her questions. She even walked out of class a couple of times. But I was determined to stay positive with her. I knew she was smart, but I had to embrace failure almost every day with that student. She made me doubt everything. Even on days when the other students were engaged, and the lesson was rocking, she would not participate. I refused to accept *absolute* failure, and spent hours fretting over how to bring this young woman into the classroom more fully. I didn't get mad at her; I was mad at myself. I kept thinking, *what am I doing wrong?*

Second, the Purposeful Hustler dissects failures. I asked myself, *what lessons can be gleaned from my failure to engage the student effectively?* I tried a lot of things with that student, and I paid close attention to how she responded. She was most upset with me when I asked her to read in front of the class, and I realized that maybe she was self-conscious about her reading. So, I started asking people to volunteer for reading instead of calling on individuals. I told the class that I was going to do that, and she started to make eye contact with me more often. She would also get mad when I called on her to ask a question. I concluded that she didn't like to be surprised and started to forewarn her when I was going to call on her. I would say, "I am going to ask you to respond to question number five, so please get ready for that one." This method seemed to work, and she began answering questions. But even with these changes, her grades were still low, and her participation was well below the other students in the class. However, dissecting the times when I was failing to engage her helped us start to turn the tide. I began to see my "failures" for what they really were: temporary setbacks that I had to work to overcome.

Third, a Purposeful Hustler re-strategizes. I realized that while my disengaged student needed more individual attention to get back on track, the classroom was not going to be the place to provide it. So, I did what any Purposeful Hustler would do and used what I had learned from my failures to create an even bolder plan. When it was time to hand out roles for the mock trial competition, I gave her a really important one. Her classmates grumbled out loud. "She isn't going to do it, Ms. Singh." "Why did you give her such an important part?" I called her mother and asked if we could work together after school. Her mother agreed, and my student was not happy. But as I suspected and had learned through my many other failures, she was much more willing to try to engage with the material when she was not with the full class, and we made a lot of progress together.

Fourth, a Purposeful Hustler keeps their end goal in sight. The Purposeful Hustler is okay with taking a risk because they know that, even in the midst of a setback, success will be greater than the sum of their failures. Even when it hurts the most, Purposeful Hustlers continue to pursue their goals. On the day of the mock trial competition, everyone piled onto the bus except her. I waited as long as I could before setting out for the courthouse. I felt crushed and was trying my best not to show this to my students, who were busy drilling another student who they had chosen to replace her.

But when we got to the courthouse, she was standing by the front door. She had gotten her hair done, was dressed to the nines, and was beaming from one side to the next. She told me she decided to get a ride because she didn't want to wrinkle her skirt. I have a picture of her classmates standing in the courtroom with their mouths wide open during her presentation at the mock trial competition. They were all so astonished by her, that they stood the entire time she was speaking. When she received an honorable mention, we all celebrated like we were taking home first place.

The next year I saw her at the school when I went back to visit the new class. She was sitting in the corner of the class and I walked up to her and gave her a sly smile. "Why are you in here? You can't take this class twice." She looked me right in the eye and said without skipping a beat, "I am here to coach them."

After having so many failures, this was a really sweet moment. One I will forever treasure. This moment is what inspired me to bring the Street Law Program to Milwaukee. It helped me remember the importance of the program and keep my goal in sight, even when the path was unclear.

Fifth, (if literally all else fails) a Purposeful Hustler admits it, learns from it, owns it, and moves on.

I love to tell this story about my Street Law student because there is a beautiful ending. But it could have gone the other way. She could have skipped the mock trial and not shown up at the courthouse. She could have proven my students right when they complained that she shouldn't have been given a big part. This begs the question: what happens when you fail, do all of the things listed in the previous steps, and then fail again? There is a chance you've made a mistake and are pushing forward in the wrong direction. It might be hard to admit when you are wrong but remember that you are human. It is okay to fail at something—just make sure to view it as a learning experience, instead of just an embarrassment.

If you are a Purposeful Hustler, the story doesn't end with failure. When you realize you've made a mistake, *admit it, learn from it, own it, and move on.*

Recently, I had a really strong idea about how a program should be designed. I presented it to my team as a demo and it fell flat. People didn't understand what I was trying to convey, so I decided to use another tactic. This second time I presented my idea, I tried to differentiate what I was proposing by putting down another organization's program. This was low and unnecessary, and it did not authentically reflect who I am. My team rejected the idea again, but this time I had also offended them.

A team member, thankfully, pointed out the damage I had done. I had violated a cultural norm of our teams and had let them down. So, what did I do? First, I admitted to myself that my approach was wrong and thanked my colleague profusely for giving me the feedback. Second, I carved out time to explore the organization I was dissing and realized that a better strategy probably would have been to highlight our commonalities. This would have been more authentic to who I am and would have made my points more comprehensible. Third, I talked to the team members who saw my presentation, personally apologized, and shared with them what I had learned about the other organization. I also sent an apology note. I was embarrassed, but I knew that as their leader I had to own my mistake. When I had finished processing it all, I moved on. I worked closely with my team to talk about how we could make the pitch better and we ended up scrapping everything and going in a different direction altogether. I learned a lot in that moment of failure.

FIND YOUR CREW

It's tough to be courageous every day of the week. When you're staring down failure and desperately trying to re-strategize, you might need to lean on others for a little support or a morale boost. Being a Purposeful Hustler is hard enough! No one said you had to do this thing on your own.

I often talk about the poster my mother bought from the 99-cent store when I was a teenager and hung on my wall. It was titled something like "100 Ways to Happiness." I don't remember anything on that list but the first thing. It said, "99% of your happiness will be determined by who you marry." I was very fortunate to marry my best friend (since 5th grade) and can attest that this guidance can be very true BUT I think the advice extends beyond one's choice of spouse. What the poster should have said is, "99% of your happiness will be determined by who you let into your crew." Your crew is who you decide to spend your precious time with. It's the people you trust and can go to, time and again, for support and guidance. Though this is not a book about relationships, I would be remiss if I didn't address just how important others can be on your path to becoming a Purposeful Hustler. You need people you can lean on when things get really hard, whether you're facing failures or overwhelmed by successes!

SO, WHERE DO I FIND THESE PEOPLE?

I recognize that I am fortunate to have a supportive family and loving husband, but even if you are not currently tied to a strong support network, you can still intentionally build this crew into your life. Here are a few things to consider when searching for people who will provide you with a soft cushion when you fall.

Look Back

You've probably failed once or twice before. When that happened, who was there? When you have identified these people, send them each a note. Try framing your message like this:

I just want to say thank you for being an awesome person in my life. I was recently reflecting on who has been there for me during some of my most trying moments, and I thought of you. I am moving into a new space, one that has me a bit freaked out. I am trying to more intentionally live in my purpose, and I am hoping to count on your support again. For the next three months, could we schedule a 30-minute call/wine/coffee each month? I just want to be able to check in with you. I so appreciate your friendship, guidance, and perspective.

Look to the Side

Who are your peers in the space you are entering? It is highly likely that some of their experiences and trials mirror yours. I developed a system where I take one-on-one walks with my peers. In the winter, we go to the nearest mall and walk inside. When the weather is nice, we take to the outdoors. I schedule about 45 minutes for these walks, and they typically happen in the morning or at the end of the day. Why the walk 'n' talks? They are valuable for (re)connecting with people working in the same space as you, and for building up your circle. These walks also make it possible to open up about whatever might be stressing you out or to celebrate recent successes. The walks are all about give and take—I always learn something and I always try to provide something. They're also a way to sneak in some exercise in addition to creating an open space for sharing and growing with your peers.

Look Ahead

Who do you admire and hope to emulate within your purpose area? Make a list. Then get online and dig around a little to see if these people truly seem to fit with the work you'd like to be doing. Look at their connections as well to see if they might be valuable connections. Then reach out and request 30 minutes of their time. When you meet, be prepared with this script outline:

o   Introduction: My purpose is to... and I see that it seems to match yours in that... I appreciate how you are already living in this space and I would love to learn from you.

o   Here are three things that I am scared of.... have you had to deal with any of these? If so, what did you do to overcome them? If not, what other challenges have you had to face?

o   As I move forward, do you have any advice for me? Anything you wish someone would have told you when you were at this point in your journey?

o   Conclude: Thank you. Would you be open to meeting again in a few months? Is there anyone else I should be talking to?

Look Across!

It is critically important to fill your circle with people who work in and understand your space, but it's also beneficial to include people who are unfamiliar with your space. A few people in my circle only vaguely understand what I do. These are people who I have met through other facets of my life—volunteering, neighborhood gatherings, travel. This group is important because Purposeful Hustlers need an occasional break from talking about the things that grip them. It's healthy to have people in your circle who are interested in other aspects of what makes you, you. Join a wine club, meetup group, crafting corner, intramural sports team—anything that touches on the other aspects of your being.

Look Inside

You are the most important person in your crew. When I am really stressed out, my husband will say to me, "Please be kind to my wife." We always laugh, because I know exactly what he means. Sometimes, the person that I need in my corner is myself. Self-care cannot be neglected. When you are pursuing your Purposeful Hustle, there will be times when you get totally lost in your flow. You will look up and realize that entire days have passed and you haven't done any of your normal daily tasks—showering, brushing your teeth, talking to other humans, eating, etc. I wish I was not as familiar with this as I am. I get lost in my Purposeful Hustle all the time. Since I know this about myself, I have created some important guardrails to keep me from falling off the face of the earth!

Here is my list:

- On weekdays I do not work between 5:00-8:00 p.m. That is family time!

- I will only attend one work event per week in the evenings.

- I must work out at least three times per week for 30 minutes. Anything on top of that is a bonus!

- I take my children on individual "dates," a time for just the two of us to connect. My husband and I have at least one date night each month.

- I prepare healthy(ish) meals on Sunday for the week so even when I am busy I have a go-to option.

- I block off entire days, weekends, and weeks that I will NOT be "on."

- I set alarms all day long to remember to take breaks.

- I make sure I am putting in time to do things I love: reading, traveling, going thrift shopping, or dancing!

- I keep an ongoing smile file. This is where I put notes, quotes, cards, or emails people have sent me. I have had one for over a decade now and have collected so many cool things. When I need a pick me up, I open the file! There is always a little treasure that helps me put things back into perspective.

Find your crew and hold on tight! Make sure these people know that they matter to you. Reconnect often, and regularly express your appreciation. Even the most resilient Purposeful Hustler needs to lean on others every once in a while.When navigating through failures, call upon your crew when necessary, but know that you are strong enough to weather many challenges on your own. Deploy techniques that embrace failure and dissect it, then re-strategize, keeping your eye on the end goal. If your attempt to fix a failure truly fails, **do your best to admit it, learn from it, own it, and move on**.

STUDY YOURSELF:

I love to ask a particular interview question: "What would be the worst thing that could happen to you if you got this new job?" This requires some fast thinking but if someone is applying for a job they have likely thought about what could go wrong, and typically have a response. Then I ask them what they would do if that terrible thing happened. No matter what they say, I respond back by saying, "Okay, let's pretend you acted in that way and it failed to work, what would you do then?" They respond, and I ask them again, "Let's pretend that did not work either. What would you do?" I keep using this same line of questions, and I tick on my paper how many times they can come up with another answer.

This question reveals a few things. First, it shows how their reflective muscles work. Second, it demonstrates how good they are at problem-solving. Third, it gives me an idea of where they hold their locus of control: internally or externally (do they talk about what they can do to solve the problem or what other people should be doing?). Fourth, it shows their persistence. A persistent person grabs hold of the challenge and will only let it go when it is clear that there isn't anything else they can do in a situation. A truly persistent person continues to work on the issue long after I have moved on to another question. Finally, the question reveals how they respond under pressure. What do they do when they are pushed out of their comfort zone?

RESILIENCY TEST

What are the worst-case scenarios that could happen if you followed your purpose?

Now, write out at least 10 ideas to potentially overcome those setbacks.

1.
2.
3.
4.
5.
6.
7.
8.
9.
10.

Active Reflection:

1. Think about the interview question that I shared. What is the worst thing that could happen when you are following your purpose?

2. What if that thing happened?

    o How would you respond?

    o What would happen if your first response failed?

    o What would happen if your second response failed?

    o How many times could you come back? See if you can get to at least ten responses!

3. Can you think of a recent failure? How might it have been handled differently using the framework of "embrace it, dissect it, and re-strategize?"

4. Who is in your crew? Who is missing and how can you add them?

5. How will you commit to improving your self-care?

CHAPTER SEVEN:
Initiative
(For the person who doesn't have it all figured out)

Nothing will work unless you do.

-Maya Angelou

W hen I ask people why they are not acting in their purpose I frequently hear some version of these three sentiments: I do not have a plan, I need more money, or I have no time.

When I hear these three issues, I get nervous. If someone continues to wait for a fully fleshed out plan, more money, and extra time, they may never start moving in their purpose. For most of us, waiting for those three things to line up perfectly is an elusive goal. Living in your purpose will require some risk-taking. Doing big things, and making big changes, requires big risk. When people have big dreams—the ones that will help them fulfill their life's purpose—but are unwilling to take any risk, there is a disconnect.

I get it. When you are trying to change the world, the question of where to start can be overwhelming. It is easier to point to the lack of a solid plan, money, or time as the reason why you can't pursue that purpose. But since you are here to be a Purposeful Hustler, let's try to eliminate all those excuses.

YOUR PLANS CAN HAVE HOLES

Planning can be a trap. I have seen this happen to countless people. They get an idea in their head about something they want to do, they sit down to write a plan, and then the plan never leaves the paper. It stays safe in its notebook, while the planner revisits it from time to time, trying to smooth out any flaws.

I am a planner. I realize how satisfying it is to have things lined up. However, in all the time I have been doing this work, no matter who was behind the plan, I have never seen anything go precisely the way people thought it would.

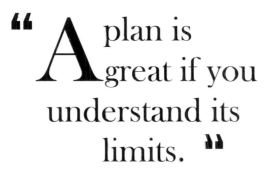

"A plan is great if you understand its limits."

It is not going to be able to position you for every contingency. It will never be complete. It will never be perfect. What a plan does is help you set your course, organize your thoughts, and develop a platform to share with others. If you recognize the merits of a plan *and* its limitations, you will be able to use it more successfully.

In my experience, the people who get lost in the allure of creating a fool-proof plan will often get stuck. To be a Purposeful Hustler, you have to learn how to trust and adapt to the things that happen organically. You'll have to learn to be nimble and pivot when the unexpected happens because sometimes your purpose will lead you into totally unexpected territory without any warning. In those moments your plan will be useless. The only thing you will need is clarity around who you are and what you are meant to do. This kind of on-your-toes thinking reminds me of one of my first fights for diversity and inclusion.

It was the third Monday in January. Earlier that morning my mother and I had argued about going to school.

"I shouldn't have to go to school today; it is a NATIONAL

holiday," I declared.

She replied, without hesitation, "Deanna, you have school today, so you are going."

I was 14 years old and a freshman in high school. I went to an almost all white school in the suburbs. As the daughter of an African American and Asian Indian, I was hyper-aware of being one of the few children of color in the entire school. I encountered a lot of cultural insensitivity growing up in that environment—being called the "N" word, hearing jokes about my father's turban, and being told to "go back to where I came from" was par for the course.

On that particular day, I felt more isolated than usual because I wasn't just facing some ignorant person making a poor judgment, I was dealing with the entire school district's neglect to acknowledge Martin Luther King Jr. Day. I sat in school all day waiting for someone to say something about the national holiday. I hoped somebody would, at the very least, play the same old video about Martin Luther King Jr. I had seen throughout elementary and middle school. Nope. My skin burned in frustration.

Earlier in the year, we had celebrated Christopher Columbus Day. Not only did we have time off from school, but many classrooms initiated conversations about Columbus and his holiday. None of those conversations included discussions about any of the foolish and deplorable activities to which Columbus subjected the Native Americans. No, he was just celebrated. Yet, here we were on the designated holiday of Martin Luther King Jr., a man who was killed because of his advocacy for civil rights in our country, and there was deafening silence. How could the school simply ignore the only national holiday honoring a person of color in our country?

With the day almost half over, I could not hear my classroom teacher over all my internal rage. I got up and walked out of class. A devoted student, this was a very unusual thing for me to do. I had no idea where I was going when I left, but I ended up in the cafeteria. It was the last period of lunch, and more than 300 of my classmates were sitting at their tables. I walked straight through the cafeteria, got up on the stage, and started reciting "The Negro Mother" by Langston Hughes in my loudest voice.

The whole cafeteria fell silent. No one tried to stop me. The staff members looked on with confusion. When I finished, I said something like, "Today is Martin Luther King Jr. Day. If you don't know who he was or why he was so important, please ask someone." From the other side of the cafeteria, a booming clap came from a football coach—the only person of color on the staff. The rest of the cafeteria, still a little stunned, started clapping too. The coach walked up on stage and grabbed my hand. It was then that I realized I was crying and shaking.

"Where are you supposed to be, Deanna?" he asked gently.

"In class."

We walked back up the stairs to class together. When we got to the door, my classroom teacher started to admonish me, "Where have you been Deanna, you can't—"

The coach stopped her. "She was with me. She did a Martin Luther King Jr. presentation. She's good now."

This sounds like a scene out of a movie, right? I wish I could say that the district changed its policy and started to honor Martin Luther King Jr. Day, but that's not what happened. What *did* happen was that my classmates started asking me a lot of questions. They wanted to know more about MLK Day. They wanted to know why I had been moved to take a stand and why this day was so important. They asked me about the poem I had recited, and if I knew any others. I talked to people I had never spoken to before.

My actions also raised awareness amongst the staff. Many of them talked to me about my impromptu speech. Faculty members started recognizing blind spots in their curriculum, not just around Martin Luther King Jr. Day, but around other gaps. The literature teacher added African American literature to his class syllabus, and I read my first novel written by a person of color that year in school. He also helped me curate a list of other books written by people of color.

I didn't start off with a plan. If I had a plan, it likely would not have been as impactful. Why? Because it was the rawness that sparked the reactions from the people around me. They could feel it, and they wanted to be a part of it.

With the gathering momentum around diversity and inclusion, I worked with others to build a plan around it. As students, we started a group called Culture Club—an organization that met after school to share different things about our cultures. We ate, danced, listened to music, watched movies, and gave students the floor to talk about their histories and countries of origin. In its first year, it became the highest attended extracurricular group in the school. Together we organized a large folk fair and ran it after school. For the folk fair, we convinced local ethnic restaurants to give us free food, we displayed things from our homes that represented our cultures, and we asked professional organizations to put on presentations. It was so powerful and well attended that our principal decided to let us do it during the school day in subsequent years so that all the students and teachers could experience it.

Marching out of that classroom, stepping onto that stage, and using my voice to spark a change within the school—even though I was a child, a student, a freshman girl, and a minority—was one of many affirmations of this important truth: You do not need permission to start change, and you do not have to have a fully fleshed out business plan. Sometimes you have to move with your gut.

I am not advocating that you do everything spontaneously. There are times when a little planning is necessary, like the example I gave in Chapter Four about creating a mitigation strategy. My advice is to make a plan when you can but remember its limitations. Plan like a Purposeful Hustler and remember:

- Plans should be flexible. You have to be willing to change as different circumstances present themselves.

- Plans will provide guidance, not unbreakable rules. You have to go in knowing that you are going to deviate from the plan.

- Having a plan is not a prerequisite for taking action. There will be times when you have to move and plan at the same time.

Your plan can give you an overarching map of where you want to go without bogging you down with details. It's like knowing that you have to get to the bank, but also having the freedom to select your mode of transportation, your arrival time, and what you'll snack on along the way. The Purposeful Hustler likes to have a plan, but they do not need it to be perfect. They aim for what will help keep them focused on their goals, but also allows them to remain nimble enough to pivot when they need to.

> **" You do not need permission to start change. "**

MONEY ON YOUR MIND

The second thing I often hear from people who are stuck outside their purpose is, "I do not have enough money to pursue my purpose." Having run multiple foundations, I can say with zero hesitation that the challenges we have in front of us require money, but it is not the lack of money that is preventing change from happening. The best question is not, "How do we get more money?" The better question is, "How can we use what we already have more effectively?"

With little or no money, I have seen people create countless impactful solutions. In fact, I soon realized in my philanthropic work that the organizations with the biggest impact are often the ones that are the most underfunded. Why? Because those organizations prioritize impact over fundraising and are too busy doing the work to raise the money. Completely neglecting fundraising is not a good business practice, but the point is, you *can* make an impact without a large cash flow. How have those organizations and individuals made an impact with limited resources? They hustle.

I signed up for a service project in the Bronx during my first week of college. My assignment was with an organization called Fordham Bedford Children Services (FBCS), a few blocks away from campus. One of the most interesting things about the campus was its location. Depending on which direction you headed, you could find yourself in the Botanical Gardens, the Bronx Zoo, Little Italy, or Fordham Road (the quintessential Bronx). Much of my work took me into the Fordham Bedford neighborhood, where FBCS supported some housing complexes. At the time, the neighborhood was mostly populated by recently immigrated Puerto Rican and Dominican families.

On my first service day, I was asked to accompany some children, between the ages of eight and twelve, on the train down to Central Park. I LOVED every minute of that trip. I was as excited as they were to be riding on the subway to Manhattan. From Fordham Road, the Central Park stop on the express train is just five stops away, and at the time, the subway fare was $1.50. It seemed to me that if you lived in such close proximity to one of the world's most well-known sites you would have seen it. But this was the first time the children had been to Central Park. Most of their parents had never been there either.

I was immediately hooked to FBCS and the children I met that day. After that initial experience, I would show up to tutor as a volunteer. Other college volunteers showed up about once a week, but not me. I was there all the time. That building felt like home. And if I was not at FBCS I was exploring NYC and all the amazing things it had to offer. I wanted to share some of that magic—the invigorating energy of the city—with the FBCS kids.

I resisted my vague ideas of taking the kids on local field trips because I perceived money to be a barrier, but I was humbled into action by a very memorable gift. One day, a parent of one of my students brought me a present. When I opened it, I was shocked to find a package of underwear and some socks. Let me pause here and clarify before your imagination goes too far: These were cotton, multi-pack, pure utility granny panties. She told me she was out buying things for her children, and thought about me, a young woman in a new city. She figured she should pick me up some essentials since my mother wasn't with me. This was a weird and unconventional thing to do, but most importantly, it was touching. I had a lot of questions going through my mind that night.

The obvious question: Why did she give me the underwear? The ridiculous question: Why did I take them? The hardest question: How could I pay her back for her kind gift? I knew she did not have a lot of disposable income and I was touched that she had used some of it on me. This was her way, I realized, of thanking me for helping her daughter with her reading.

I came back to FBCS with a different attitude. I took a page from the mother's book, and instead of waiting to be told what I should do, I started looking around for what I could do. It was that shift in thinking that gave me the courage to go and talk to the Executive Director and ask if I could start a new program. The mother had noticed that I was in NYC by myself. She had, with her limited resources, found a way to make me feel special. But I had noticed something too. You see, I had noticed that the FBCS students, though they were living in NYC, knew nothing about their own city. Most of them were first-generation Dominican or Puerto Rican, and they had spent most of their time within a six-block radius. To me, this seemed like such a missed opportunity because they were in NYC!

I told the Executive Director that if he gave me $500, breakfast, lunch, and subway tokens, I could take 30 students ages 8-12, on four field trips a week for six weeks. That was 24 field trips.

Anyone who has gone on an outing with children can tell you that it is very easy to spend $500 with just a handful of kids on one outing, so this seemed like a ridiculous idea. I will never know why he said yes, but I am so glad he did.

During the summer between my Freshman and Sophomore year, I would get onto subway trains four times each week. I would hold the car doors open and yell, "I am about to bring 30 kids onto this car, just in case you want to move to the next one." This almost always got us enough seats to make sure everyone could sit down. Then we would create an assembly line of food, drinks, and cleaning supplies. We never left a thing or, thankfully, a child behind! The 30 children, a few high school helpers, and I wandered around the city together having all kinds of adventures. We called it Bronx and Beyond.

Because I did not have any money, our field trips were awkward at times. I remember one time, in particular, I had the parents bring in their children very early. I wanted to be the first in line at an awesome museum. This museum was crazy expensive (I couldn't even afford to buy myself a ticket!), but I knew the students wanted to see it. When the museum opened, and the guard came to let us in, she pulled the rope and said, "Tickets please." I leaned in and whispered, "I don't have any tickets." She promptly responded, "I'm sorry, but you can't get in without tickets." I responded, "No problem, but do you mind telling the kids that?" She looked over my shoulder and then stepped to the side to let us in. Good thing, because I didn't have a plan B.

Receiving that underwear is something I will never forget. With very little money, the mother made a tremendous impression on me—she showed me that you don't have to be made of money to make a difference. She decided to spend the little she had on me, and it made a huge impact. Her initiative and selflessness inspired me to take initiative.

At times, it might be hard to find money to fulfill your purpose. You may even have to exchange goodwill instead of dollars. However, you might be surprised by how far you can get with very little. When I think back on all the initiatives I have started while following my purpose, I was typically under-resourced at first. In most instances, "under-resourced" meant I had access to less than a few hundred dollars, or sometimes nothing at all. What I did have was an abundance of sweat equity, people who were moved by the vision and willing to help, and innovative, cost-effective ways to get things done.

What does that look like in practice? Well, beyond guilting security guards into letting in the children for free, I also used a few other Purposeful Hustler tactics. Please note: A Purposeful Hustler uses resources creatively but is NOT exploitative. Make sure your actions are rooted in doing good, rather than used for leveraging others for personal gain. In this case, all my actions revolved around creating positive experiences for children. I came up with many tactics, like when I:

- **Wrote moving letters** to the owners of different places and had the children sign them.

- **Pled in person** (it is harder to say no to someone's face); when I could not get people to return my calls, I would just show up.

- Found **people that were connected** to FBCS, myself, or to the places we wanted to visit. Could someone from my university help out? An alum? A co-worker's spouse? A donor?

- **Became creative with the goal**. I looked up interesting people and asked if they would just meet with us. These people became our destinations!

- **Went off the beaten path** and found things that were odd, like a random junkyard sculpture garden. The curators were thrilled to have visitors and not complainers!

- **Asked** organizations if they had any money set aside for groups like ours that couldn't afford their services outright. Don't underestimate the power of just asking.

- **Cold-called** places and explained what I was trying to do.

- Went to **free** places like iconic parks and statues.

- Was **extra savvy with coupons and group discounts!**

I could go on, but as you look at this list, I hope you can see that we were able to accomplish a lot with a little. Any one of these techniques could be applied to other circumstances. The underlying message is that the Purposeful Hustler (1) thinks non-traditionally about how to get things done and (2) is not too proud to ask for help, be scrappy, or be vulnerable. When people understand what you are doing and why they will try to find a way to help you. We are built that way.

"BUT I'M SO BUSY!"

Another common roadblock for people who feel stuck operating outside of their purpose is that they are not able to fit purpose work into their schedules. The problem with this mindset is that your purpose should always be close to the top of your priority box, if not the top thing. We live in a world where many things vie for our attention or require our responsibility. We work, care for our families, attend to civic and social duties, and much more. Sometimes, pursuing our purpose can seem like just another thing.

I often use one simple strategy when I feel like I am too overwhelmed to follow where purpose is leading me: **I do one thing every day that will help me stay aligned—or get realigned—with my purpose. I move.**

At the age of seven, my son gave me a powerful reminder of just how much can be accomplished by dedicating a short amount of time to a project, every single day. The idea for his project came about one day while he was leaning over my shoulder, reading an article I had pulled up on my computer. The article was about a group of local community members in Seattle who decided to host a world dance party. The idea was simple: they hosted a potluck at a community center and got professional dancers to donate 15 minutes of their time to teach everyone how to do a different ethnic dance. With all of his seven-year-old wisdom, my son said:

"Hey, we love eating, learning about different cultures, and dancing. What if I start the same thing in our city?"

I looked into his eyes and realized right away he was serious. "Of course," I replied.

"But mom, one difference." He paused. "I want ours to be an EPIC World Dance Party."

In the back of my head I was thinking, *when in the world are we going to find time to do this EPIC party?* We already had a really busy schedule, and one more thing could tip us over the edge. But then I decided to add this to my purpose-centered calendaring system.

The next day, with an even more excited son, we made a list of all of the things we needed to do to make the EPIC World Dance Party happen. It took about ten minutes to list the steps we felt we needed to take.

From that point, we tried to do something on the list almost every morning before heading to work or school. We rarely spent more than ten minutes a day on our list (a testament to how much can be achieved if things are tackled in consistent, bite-sized chunks). For example, one of the tasks my son accomplished one morning was calling the Executive Director of the community center to see if it was possible to use their space. He said yes, and also waived the rental fee since we were not looking to raise any money from the event. Additionally, he gave us the name of a dance instructor and a D.J. to contact. Another morning, my son called a salsa teacher he knew and asked if he would join the fun. He also said yes, and gave us a list of other dancers to contact. We then drafted a flyer (which the marketing department of the community center spruced up a bit) and went to social media to start sharing information about the event. I gave my son a $100 budget to cover decorations and basic food items. He ordered some decorations online and made the others. On the invitations, he noted that this was a potluck and encouraged people to bring their favorite cultural foods to share. He also made some very intentional calls to some family members to request special dishes!

When the day of the event came, over 125 people attended. My favorite quotes included: "He (my son) should run for President—this was a great way to bring the community together," "I have never seen an event with this much diversity in all aspects—age and race—in all the years I have lived in this city, and I am in my 40s," and "Wow, I didn't realize my body could move like that! I can't wait until next year!"

And when the next year came, my son did it again. The second time, he planned the party with his then four-year-old brother. The EPIC World Dance Party has since become an annual tradition and an excellent example of what can be accomplished over the course of a few weeks by working for about ten minutes a day. Through a small commitment of time, you can still make a big impact. Even in our busy adult lives, we can all find at least ten minutes every day to commit ourselves to our purpose.

How To Calendar with Purpose!

To make time for the things that matter, I keep purpose at the forefront of my calendar system. Most of us are juggling many things—work, school, family, health—so intentionally setting aside time is crucial for getting purpose-centered work accomplished. I use purpose-driven calendaring in order to get things done. When I calendar with purpose, I typically follow three steps:

Step One: Annual Prep

Annual Prep Overview: Each year, I set aside two or three days to reflect and plan. One of those days is completely dedicated to reflecting on my purpose and thinking about how I can go deeper in the upcoming year (the other days are used for logistical tasks like budgeting, calendaring, etc.). During my annual prep session a few years ago, against a backdrop of a lot of national divisiveness, I decided that I wanted to get on a larger stage to talk about why it is important to build bridges with one another. I immediately thought about trying to get on a TEDx stage. The only thing I did during my annual planning was finding the application date. Then I worked backward and thought about what I needed to accomplish during each month leading up to the application deadline:

- Month 1: Outline completed

- Month 2: Rough Draft Started

- Month 3: Rough Draft Completed

- Month 4: Test Rough Draft & Make a Video

- Month 5: Final Application Submitted!

Step Two: Create Bite-Sized Tasks

Two weeks before the end of every quarter, I set aside a day to review what has happened in the quarter and to plan for the next quarter. During this time, I get way more granular. Thinking about my TEDx application, I knew that my goals in the first quarter were to complete the outline and rough draft. Understanding that, I dissected the months into weeks. For example, this is what the first month looked like:

Month One

- Week One: List all the ways I could address my desired topic

- Week Two: Go through old notes and see what information resonates with people during individual conversations

- Week Three: Draft the outline based on learnings from weeks one and two

- Week Four: Add personal stories into the outline that will help exemplify the topic

If I had not set up this time during my annual planning, the thought of applying for the TEDx talk would have remained just a thought. It would have felt too daunting and I would not have had the time to prepare for it appropriately.

Step Three: Build a Model Schedule with Daily Priorities
This is how I organize my days:

- Before my feet hit the ground in the morning, I decide what 1-3 things I want to accomplish that day. I try to make sure that the list is something that is achievable and focused on greater purpose.

- Each day has a priority focus. For example, every Monday I work on Purposeful Strategy. That means things on my task list in that Purposeful Strategy category get pulled to the top of my to-do pile.

- Each day is then chunked into major commitments. Some categories repeat almost every day:

  o **Daily Prep & Prayer**: I wake up around 5:30 every morning, but I don't get out of bed until around 6:00. During that time I come up with my top three priorities for the day, pray, and often cuddle with my family and talk about what they have coming up in the day.

  o **Family Chores**: Outside of sitting down for breakfast with my family and helping my children get off to their days, this is when I pay bills, do laundry, clean out cabinets that are irritating me, respond to invitations, etc.

  o **Exercise**: I build workout time into my calendar at least three mornings per week.

DEANNA SINGH

o **Admin**: At the end of my work day, I respond to email, clean up tasks for the day, and get ready for the next day.

o **Family Time**: During this time, I try to put away my computer and phone. We cook, eat together, play games, whatever we feel like! After my children are asleep this is also the time my husband and I hang out.

o **Purpose Time**: I have the extreme luxury of making this block as large or small as I want to because I am running my own company. However, I had this block even when I had far less control over my time. This time can be as short as five minutes and up to hours. My simple rule is to do at least one thing every day that falls within purpose. That might mean sending an email or pulling up an article I have been meaning to read and skimming it before going to bed. I dream about the day when ALL of my unallocated time is spent on purpose!

In addition to these daily chunks, I also incorporate three free periods into my day. I keep a running list of things I could do during those free periods in a "model schedule." This model schedule is something I review during my annual/quarterly check-ins because it has to change to reflect different seasons. To see an interactive version of this model and download your own fillable copy, visit the resources page on my website, www.deannasingh.com.

I use a paper copy of my model schedule weekly and carry it with me because it is really nice to see everything in one place, but I manage my actual tasks with technology, principally through a project management app called Nozbe. Nozbe follows the *Getting Things Done* book by David Allen, which is a great organizational book and has helped me lay a foundation for my own systems.

Here is what I love about Nozbe and why I use it every single day:

- It allows me to prioritize purposeful work.

- All of my projects/tasks can go into Nozbe, including the ones I get through email, on the web, or that I just enter directly.

- It is synced with both my phone and computer.

- I can easily see all that is going on and communicate with team members.

- It helps me judge what I can realistically get done and what needs to move.

- It helps me stay nimble but still focused.

- It helps me juggle the many different things I might have going on at any given time.

Here is a REALLY important note: My system is not flawless. It works for me about 80% of the time and, in fact, I only aim for an 80% success rate. I expect that there will be weeks, months, and sometimes quarters when I do not even reach the 80% goal. Why do I aim for just 80%, and why am I okay with occasionally missing that goal? This could be characterized as failure, but I think it is freedom because I don't want to get so bogged down in systems, even the ones that I have created, that I don't get anything done. This can be its own trap. I know that if I achieve about an 80% success rate, I will have accomplished the most important things. The 80% goal allows me to keep adjusting. I suggest that you give yourself this freedom and flexibility.

The Purposeful Hustler has the same challenges as everyone else. They are struggling to think through a fantastic plan, figure out the capital, and find the time. The difference is that they don't wait for it to come to them. Purposeful Hustlers are not passive participants in their lives. They take initiative. They go out with what they have and build from there. They use organic momentum in their favor to help build the plan, they get creative with their resources, and they keep moving every day by intentionally acting, even in small ways, to fulfill their purpose.

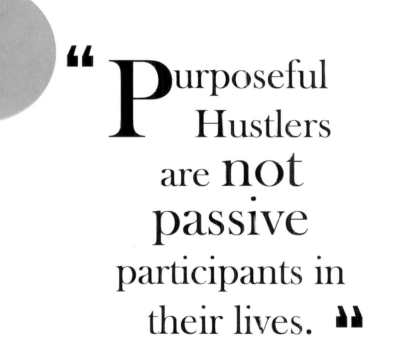

" **P**urposeful Hustlers are not passive participants in their lives. "

ACTIVE REFLECTION:

1. Does not having a plan freak you out? Try to do something completely impromptu today and see how it goes. Build up your confidence that, yes, you can act within your purpose without a set plan.

2. Can you think of one single action that you could take today that would jump start you toward your purpose?

3. If money is your hang up, make a budget that shows what you would need to make a purposeful move. Remember this should be the very bare-bones of what you would need.

4. Think of five ways you can make an impact in your particular area of interest that does NOT involve money.

5. Put 15 minutes on your calendar and commit to accomplishing one purpose-related thing every day for 30 days.

6. Write your own model schedule, or better yet, set aside a day to plan around your purpose!

15 MINUTES A DAY ON PURPOSE

What can you accomplish in just 15 minutes a day? (These can be standalone tasks or parts of a larger project).	
1	16
2	17
3	18
4	19
5	20
6	21
7	22
8	23
9	24
10	25
11	26
12	27
13	28
14	29
15	30

Next Steps

When I stand before God at the end
of my life, I would hope that I would
not have a single bit of talent left,
and could say, 'I used everything you
gave me'.

–Erma Bombeck

A re you feeling motivated? Are you ready to bring your purpose to life with a strategic hustle?

It is my sincere hope that this book has given you the tools, mindset, and inspiration you need to start living in your purpose.

Now, it's up to you. Your personal wealth of talents, skills, and resources are waiting to be tapped into and used to make meaningful changes in the world. Instead of feeling a vague sense of purpose, hopefully, you're now more focused and have a greater understanding of how to call upon a deliberate, conscientious hustle to activate your purpose.

At this point, you've had a chance to actively reflect on your own personal calling and consider how purpose can be a driving force in your life. In **Chapter One**, we explored the meaning of purpose, why it is important, the benefits of identifying one's purpose, and how to reveal it.

Chapter Two took a deeper dive and focused on how to define your personal purpose. If your purpose—the driving force behind everything you do—is left undefined, you may find it difficult to point your compass in the right direction and make crucial decisions. Have you taken the time to actively reflect on your purpose? Of the reflection methods covered in the chapter, which one(s) work best for you? It's incredibly important to consciously set aside time to explore your purpose, and later, to test it "in the field" and see how it holds up.

DEANNA SINGH

It is essential to have a "why" behind everything you do, but it's just as essential to have a "how." How will you live in your purpose? How will you achieve those big, lofty goals? **Chapter Three** introduced the concept of hustle, specifically having a *purposeful* hustle that revolves around courage, curiosity, resilience, and an action-oriented mentality. It also discussed the benefits of pairing your hustle with your purpose.

But what if you're afraid of losing your title, prestige, or the comfort of your current standing? No one said being a Purposeful Hustler is easy! **Chapter Four** demonstrated how to build reservoirs of courage and tap into them when necessary. In this chapter, we explored how to create fear mitigation strategies, as well as how to stomp out fear in the moment.

Some of our fear may stem from the belief that we do not have the required knowledge or skills to enact change. **Chapter Five** delved into this fear and discussed potential steps to overcome it, including recognizing what you already know, closing your knowledge and skill gaps, asking for help, and strengthening your intellect.

It can take a lot of work to confront your fears and press forward in your purpose. That's why one of the most important qualities of a Purposeful Hustler is relentlessness. In **Chapter Six**, that quality is discussed through the lens of failure. What happens when you face a setback? Do you reframe your strategy and try again? Or give up? In most cases, the Purposeful Hustler can overcome perceived obstacles if they are resilient and resourceful. However, in some circumstances, failure cannot be avoided and it is up to Purposeful Hustlers to pick themselves up, swallow a bit of pride, and keep moving forward with their purpose as a guide.

Failure can be scary. I get that. But you can't use the fear of failure as an excuse to never get started on your path to making a positive impact. Even if you do not have a well-developed plan, you're lacking money, or you're feeling short on time, you can still live in your purpose. **Chapter Seven** addressed these three common excuses for not living a purposeful life (lack of a plan, money, and time), and dismantled the assumptions many of us carry about our personal resources. It also demonstrated how to move forward in your purpose with an incomplete plan, little money, and scarce time by providing real and immediately applicable techniques.

So, what do you do with all this new information? How do you tie all the purpose- and hustle-related lessons together and begin walking in your purpose? You may be feeling overwhelmed, or you may be wondering, *Where on earth do I begin?*

Since everyone's journey is different, I recommend starting wherever you feel compelled to start. Maybe you need more work on defining your life's purpose. Maybe you need to build up your confidence to make a major life change. Or, maybe you need to look your excuses in the face and say, "I see you and I *will* overcome you." No matter where you start, remember to always return to your purpose and let that be the force that propels you into action and guides each decision you make.

Remember: Your purpose drives your hustle; your hustle gives shape to your purpose. You need both if you want to make a significant impact. No matter your cause, you *will* be successful if you make a concerted effort to position yourself at the intersection of purpose and hustle.

Just imagine, what would happen if you lived in your

PURPOSEFUL
HUSTLE?

How could YOU change the world?

I can't wait to see what you do!